PALEO

Eudald Carbonell, Cinta S. Bellmunt
& María Ángeles Torres

PALEO

Recipes from the Cavemen's Cookbook

Abbreviations and Quantities

1 oz = 1 ounce = 28 grams
1 lb = 1 pound = 16 ounces
1 cup = approx. 5–8 ounces* (see below)
1 cup = 8 fluid ounces = 250 milliliters (liquids)
2 cups = 1 pint (liquids) = 15 milliliters (liquids)
8 pints = 4 quarts = 1 gallon (liquids)
1 g = 1 gram = 1/1000 kilogram = 5 ml (liquids)
1 kg = 1 kilogram = 1000 grams = 2¼ lb
1 liter = 1000 milliliters (ml) = 1 quart
125 milliliters (ml) = approx. 8 tablespoons = ½ cup
1 tbsp = 1 level tablespoon = 15–20 g* (depending on density) = 15 milliliters (liquids)
1 tsp = 1 level teaspoon = 3–5 g* (depending on density) = 5 ml (liquids)

*The weight of dry ingredients varies significantly depending on the density factor, e.g. 1 cup of flour weighs less than 1 cup of butter. Quantities in ingredients have been rounded up or down for convenience, where appropriate. Metric conversions may therefore not correspond exactly. It is important to use either American or metric measurements within a recipe.

Original title: *RECETAS PALEO. LA DIETA DE NUESTROS ORÍGENES PARA UNA VIDA SALUDABLE*
ISBN 978-84-480-2206-8

© of the text: Eudald Carbonell and Cinta S. Bellmunt, 2015
© of the photographs: María Ángeles Torres, 2015
© Original idea and edition, Zahorí de Ideas (www. Zahorideideas.com), 2015
English translation rights arranged through Manuela Kerkhoff – International Licensing Agency, Germany,
www.manuela-kerkhoff.de

Design and typesetting: Mot
Adaptation of the recipes: Rico Ponti and Diana Novell
Cooking: Rico Ponti. Restaurante La Ü de Vilaür (Ampurdán)
Stylist: María Ángeles Torres
Copy editing: Diana Novell

© for this English edition: h.f.ullmann publishing GmbH

Translation from Spanish: Matthew Clarke in association with First Edition Translations Ltd, Cambridge, UK
Typesetting: Paul Barrett in association with First Edition Translations Ltd, Cambridge, UK

Coverphotos: María Ángeles Torres

Overall responsibility for production: h.f.ullmann publishing GmbH, Potsdam, Germany

Printed in Poland, 2016

ISBN 978-3-8480-0940-4

10 9 8 7 6 5 4 3 2 1
X IX VIII VII VI V IV III II I

www.ullmann-publishing.com
newsletter@ullmann-publishing.com
facebook.com/hfullmann
twitter.com/hfullmann_int

CONTENTS

INTRODUCTION

The diet of human primates has undergone enormous changes since the emergence of the *Homo* genus (the first belonging to the hominid species) in Africa 2.8 million years ago. Our ancestors were originally vegetarian and then became omnivores, and their odyssey has bequeathed to today's *Homo sapiens* a wealth of information on the living systems of the Earth and their nutritional value. During our evolutionary journey we have made use of both the animal and vegetable kingdoms to establish our diet (along with the consumption of water). We have not only taken full advantage of their nutritional properties but we have also experimented with them to create environments different than those found in the natural world.

It is important to note, therefore, that when we refer to the paleo diet we have to consider gathering as well as hunting. There is some confusion on this matter. We often picture prehistoric hunters solely as consumers of animal matter but this is not the case. Studies conducted on these populations indicate that they ate a wide range of plants, roots, fruit, stalks, flowers, and leaves. So, when we talk about the paleo diet we should think in terms of omnivores.

On the basis of fossils found on archeological sites, as well as the data derived from advances in scientific methods and increasingly sophisticated and precise technology, we have abundant information on the types of food eaten by the hominids of the Paleolithic Era. Sometimes we have direct evidence, whether from fossilized seeds that can subsequently be identified, or from animal bones that have clearly been handled by human beings. Furthermore, the remains of animals often reveal the characteristics of their natural habitat and indicate the types of plants, shrubs, and trees that would have been present. Palynological and paleocarpological analyses, along with measurements of the proportion of carbon 13 in skeletal remains, have enabled us to discover the dominant plant species in a particular setting and ascertain whether these were primarily trees or shrubs or a range of grasses.

Scientific studies of diet are therefore multidisciplinary and embrace both data obtained from the direct examination of fossils (phytolites, pollen, etc.) and other methods that provide indirect evidence, such as the analysis of tooth wear, which can be correlated with a particular type of plant or meat.

Consequently, we can deduce, for example, that the consumption of vegetables, including mushrooms (coprophages), must have been basic to the development of Paleolithic cultures, which passed on their knowledge to Neolithic societies, which in their turn mastered the secrets of fermentation and many other processes for transforming food. This gave rise to bread, beer, wine, and so on (although none of these concerns us here as these products came after the paleo diet).

THE APPEARANCE OF TECHNOLOGY

The advent of technology (i.e. stone tools) developed by the first hominids around 2.8 million years ago triggered changes in their eating habits. In fact, it marked a before and after situation—and it has played a crucial role ever since. The creation of artifacts led to new techniques for obtaining animal biomass and therefore exploiting its potential more fully. Our ancestors could take advantage of the bodies of dead animals, which they were previously unable to eat owing to limitations in their anatomy, such as lack of claws and teeth to equip them to tear meat. They could consume bone marrow and steal the spoils of other scavengers, such as hyenas and vultures, by beating them off with sticks (an example of cooperation between hominids).

Tools, whether made of stone or wood (staffs, diggers, etc.), gave them access to the subsoil—by allowing them to unearth bulbs and roots—and to the nests of insects such as ants.

It is therefore evident that technology is largely responsible for the evolution of our diet. Without it we, like our forebears, would be confined to our own physical resources, and our menu would be severely restricted as a consequence. In their journey to the present day, the various species belonging to the *Homo* genus have spent hundreds of thousands of years adapting to their environment while eating, like all omnivores, both meat and vegetable matter. In the early days they basically fed on fruits and leaves, although they also ate insects and other members of the animal kingdom. The food that the human population has consumed over its long evolution has come to us by land, sea, and air. All kinds of animal have formed part of our diet: earthbound and seafaring, vertebrates and invertebrates, birds and insects.

BY LAND, SEA, AND AIR

The totality of the thousands of human cultures that have existed, whether now extinct or still in existence, presents a mind-boggling diversity of food. It is fair to say that there is virtually no non-toxic substance that has never been eaten, from the tiniest animal to the biggest. Every part of a large animal may be put to use, although in some cases only the choicest parts are eaten. Insects are widely eaten, even today, due to their abundance and the great supply of energy derived from their high protein content. They constitute a food source of exceptional quality in hot climates.

Habitat also plays an extremely important role in diet. Climate change drove our ancestors to leave the vastness of the African forests and colonize other settings, such as more temperate woodland and shrubby savannas. These successive transformations in the ecosystem were probably another determining factor in the evolution of our diet. The savanna was a more open space, and hence more dangerous, but it also offered great opportunities to extend the food spectrum. All the *Homo* species have been omnivorous and over the course of their evolution they have modified their diet by adapting to climate change and the specific latitudes in which they have found themselves.

FEEDING THE BRAIN

The changes triggered by hominids' adaptation to more open environments led to a need to incorporate animal protein into their diet. They learned from predators how to hunt and started eating more meat. This sparked alterations in the human body as processing animal protein is completely different than metabolizing vegetable produce. Meat represented a greater input of calories and proteins, even when eaten in smaller quantities than vegetables. Meat is what makes us human. The researcher Leslie Aiello posits that when meat intake became habitual, our innards became shorter, leaving more energy for our brain to grow. This enabled our digestive system to evolve quickly. We moved from a large intestinal apparatus resembling that of gorillas and other primates to a smaller one, because our diet was no longer primarily vegetarian and we no longer needed to digest large amounts of stalks, fruits, roots, and leaves.

This represented a huge evolutionary leap, as it allowed the brain—the hardest organ for us to maintain—to grow progressively. Accordingly, the effort once devoted to digesting vegetable matter was diverted to nourishing our brains. This transformation, coupled with the use of tools, enhanced our operative intelligence, thereby diversifying our spectrum of behavior to an extent far beyond that of other species. This was the start of the adventure of the human omnivore because from then on the various species of the *Homo* genus have been generalists.

Homo sapiens, our species, consumes any digestible food within reach, and for 99.9% of its existence has been characterized by hunting and gathering. It is only in the last 8,000–10,000 years that we have turned into farmers and livestock breeders, and although we have not entirely given up on hunting, more often than not it is now a leisure activity. It is only very recently that we started eating bread, and even more recently oil, wine, and beer. All the techniques used to mimic the fermentation found in nature are modern acquisitions. We have been drinking milk for only a few thousand years because before that our bodies could not assimilate lactose.

Fire may have marked a turning point in human gastronomy because through its use food became easier to digest. Among other things, it allowed the properties of foodstuffs to be chemically modified. Fire's capacity to transform and eliminate toxins exponentially increased our forebears' spectrum of consumption and thus expanded their diet. They began to incorporate rhizomes and other underground plants, for example, because fire deactivated their toxicity.

FIRE: A TURNING POINT

Food has been cooked in any number of ways. We have transformed ingredients by boiling them, or by griddling them over a fire or on a hot stone, and then we have gone on to season them. This process involves the use of various types of support. Our ancestors would have used wood, stone (slate, schist), leaves, skins, and ovens (which have been excavated).

Nevertheless, it should be emphasized that many of the species belonging to the *Homo* genus ate cold food—not because they rejected the technology of fire but because they lacked the knowledge or technical backup required to master it. In fact, the history of humanity is the history of cold food, with plants and meat eaten systematically straight after being picked or killed. Cooking only appeared a million years ago, when fire came under human control. So, when we talk of the paleo diet, the diet of the first hominids, we must distinguish between the diets existing before and after the use of fire.

Sometime in the past, our ancestors noticed that natural fires wreaked havoc in the natural world. Fire killed animals that could not escape its advance, but these were preserved and edible, thanks to the skin protecting their flesh. Some prehistoric pioneers must have realized that fire was an element of conservation, and they must surely also have observed that smoke prevented the laying and growth of larvae in animal cadavers. These were the first steps towards smoking and preserving meat. Similarly, in hot and humid areas, when bones, meat, or plants happened to fall into warm water they changed their state. They were then eaten, inspiring cooking methods that later went on to become widespread.

Going back to fire, this brought our forebears together and made us eat together communally for the first time. Of all the animal species, only human primates practice collective eating, and this spirit of cooperation may have been apparent in activity leading to the capture of a prey. This is illustrated by the research conducted by an American scientist, the late Glynn Isaac, on the Lower Pleistocene site on the shores of Lake Turkana in the Koobi Fora region of Kenya, known for finds of hippopotamus bones and artifacts. Archeological researchers dug up the remains of a hippopotamus along with a series of stone tools dating back over a million years. Isaac hypothesized that the vertebrate would have been eaten by a group of hominids, and that this operation would have required a collective effort to dismember the animal, a form of mutual aid to get things done by group energy and socialize.

FEASTS AND BANQUETS

The sharing and eating of an animal led to celebrations and banquets in tribal societies and ceremonial gatherings in later civilizations. Food became more than something that enabled us to survive and reproduce as soon as it began to be used as a mechanism for socialization and intergenerational integration.

In the example mentioned above it was a hippopotamus that was eaten. The range of animals that served for human consumption in prehistoric times also included bison, mammoths, horses, aurochs, tigers, lions, hyenas, bears, elephants, deer, and donkeys.

OPEN-AIR FRIDGE

The preservation of food is another aspect that must be taken into account. The cold typical of northern climes spurred human beings into action. They realized that icy temperatures maintained the properties of animal cadavers. This meant that they could be preserved for long periods, and their meat could be removed and used once it had thawed. Large accumulations of mammoth bones suggest that the death of animals, maybe from hunting, allowed a community to enjoy a secure and sustained supply of protein. These animals could be stored in a settlement, and part of their meat could be defrosted by fire and eaten by the whole group, allowing members to remain in one spot for some time. The ability to store meat—whether as a result of the opportunistic discovery of several dead animals or of systematic hunting—represented a highly significant evolutionary advance. When the cold was not so intense, hominids probably learned how to smoke meat in order to preserve it, thereby replacing low temperatures with high ones as a means of adaptation.

While this progress was being made in continental systems, in coastal areas drying—oxidation by air—allowed meat to be preserved for days or even months, as did salting. Salting had a similar effect as its dehydrating properties enhanced the conservation of both land and sea animals.

THE PALEO DIET

All this took place in prehistory, before eating habits were altered by socialized technology. In our times in the throes of a scientific and technical revolution, it is inappropriate to rigidly follow the diet that was proper to hominids under constant stress from an extremely hostile environment. The members of those societies spent most of their time in the open air, which is a very different situation from ours. These days nobody panics because of being chased by a saber-toothed tiger and the functioning of our brain and metabolism has adapted, through natural selection, to a different world. Today most human beings have gone beyond the Industrial Revolution. There are only a very few groups that sustain themselves with the paleo diet, and even they are coming to the end of a road in terms of their behavior and food consumption.

In our opinion, in these times the paleo diet is a cultural adaptation. This does not mean that it cannot enhance our eating habits, but it is ultimately an anachronism. This circumstance should not, however, prevent a series of food combinations from being appreciated in gastronomic terms and enjoyed from time to time, while also enabling us to broaden our cultural horizons. Combining animals that existed in the remote past, and still exist now, with plants with the same longevity offers an enthralling way to eat. Nevertheless, we reiterate that these recipes should not be adopted on a systematic basis in a modern world in which the scientific–technical revolution is increasingly consolidating itself.

We are not in favor of the excesses associated with dogmatic views of the world, nor do we support the notion that any time in the past was better than our own. We are sensitive to cultural changes and to the new awareness evident on our planet, but we consider that the excesses of an unstructured paleo diet make no sense in the age of nanotechnology and holistic thinking.

There are some enormous differences between the dietary habits of prehistoric hominids and our own. In today's world, saturated fats are not effectively assimilated by the body and if they—or sugars—are eaten in excess they can be very harmful. All too often, overeating of these foods, coupled with the sedentary habits of *Homo sapiens,* far removed from the continuous exercise of hunter-gatherers, results in obesity. This impedes the general functioning of the body as excess weight can cause problems in movement and damage joints and muscles.

THE PALEO DIET TODAY

A sensibly managed paleo diet can therefore have benefits. It can also be fun, as we hope to demonstrate in the recipes below. There is something for everybody, and for every time of day.

Vegetables are enormously important in the paleo diet. Always try to buy the freshest you can find—or, better still, whenever possible grow them yourself or forage for them in the countryside, as our ancestors used to do. Whether cooked or raw, they are always a good source of fiber. They are also delicious and extremely healthy, and they can be eaten alone, in combination, or as an accompaniment to other kinds of food.

As for protein, make sure that it is of high quality and as organic as possible, derived from animals raised in natural settings and under healthy conditions, free of all growth-enhancing fodder. And take advantage of all their body parts: meat, tripe, eggs, and so on.

Fancy an afternoon's fishing? Why not? Catching your own fish is extremely enjoyable—not to mention cooking and savoring it afterward. If you share these pleasures they become all the more delightful. First, check that fishing is permitted where and when you plan to go, and that you are aware of any species that are protected. Then you can head for the country with a group of friends to gather your ingredients and prepare and eat them together. Furthermore, fresh air helps us obtain vitamin D, which we need in abundance. (Alongside direct sunlight, egg yolks, blue fish, and offal are recommended sources of vitamin D.)

Let us not forget aromatic herbs and spices. They enhance the flavor of salads, meat, and fish, while also providing a good dose of antioxidants. Many herbs also have medicinal properties—thyme, rosemary, and mint, for example. Nuts also need to be included in our diet. Walnuts, filberts, and pine nuts are all extremely beneficial in health terms. They help to control cholesterol and maintain good circulation, they strengthen the heart, and they slow the advance of degenerative diseases. They also provide vitamins, along with minerals such as phosphorus, calcium, potassium, copper, iron, and selenium.

So, adapting our diet to the practices of our prehistoric forebears can help us stay healthy, as well as allowing us to have a good time cooking food—and eating it. The paleo diet will tickle the palate! We have supplied two versions of our recipes: the first for you to follow and the second to show what our ancestors would have done.

COOKING METHODS

The paleo diet draws on natural produce, basically animals and plants, which can be treated with heat or eaten raw. Cooking food goes back hundreds of thousands of years. The first known experiments with fire took place around 1 million years ago, in the Wonderwerk Cave in South Africa.

The consumption of natural produce by humankind forms part of the tradition of omnivorous mammals— those that eat both meat and vegetables. The ability to make use of fire totally changed the human diet as this technological innovation ushered in a whole new range of ingredients. Over time, the different ways of using fire would transform the eating practices of the first prehistoric settlers.

Fire can be used in various ways to preserve and cook food, the most common being these:

- Fire made with wood from natural surroundings. If possible, the produce itself should come from the same area. This includes plants, which should be native species. A fire is lit with wood, twigs, and leaves from shrubs or trees and the food is placed directly on the embers, or it can be cooked without any direct contact with the flames, by hanging it above to take advantage of the heat.

- A more sophisticated method involves the use of hot stones. A fire is lit in the same way and three stones are assembled as a trilithon (a structure like a small dolmen, with two vertical stones supporting a third in a horizontal position). Food is cooked indirectly, without touching the fire, by being placed on the top stone.

- Hot stones can be used to heat liquids. They are first heated in the fire and then transferred to the liquid while still burning hot. Hot stones can also be used to cook food, by placing them under and directly on top of the ingredients.

- The tripod was another prehistoric cooking utensil. A fire was lit on the ground and three wooden sticks were stuck into the ground around it. These crossed each other above the fire and food could be hung from this meeting point, to be boiled or smoked.

- Earth ovens were made to cook food by reduction. A pit was dug in the ground and tinder wood was placed inside it. A fire was lit and once it was smoldering food was placed on top of it and covered. The pit was then filled in and the food was left to cook slowly.

RECIPES
NOTE

In order to adapt the dishes in these recipes (both raw and cooked) to contemporary tastes, we can take advantage of the fact that we live in the 21st century and have a vast array of spices at our disposal that we can add when no condiment is specified. We can also use melted fats, vegetable oils, and salt.

These touches will add flavor to paleo recipes that might otherwise prove insipid to our modern palates. We have chosen not to include such ingredients in any of our recipes as they were not used in the Paleolithic Era and therefore should not feature in a strict paleo diet. We have also refrained from using herbs and other types of garnish that certainly were used, but not frequently and only in specific areas.

The paleo diet will tickle the palate! We have supplied two versions of our recipes: the first for you to follow and the second to show what our ancestors would have done. Note that you should follow the first version of each recipe. The second shows you how our prehistoric forebears would have prepared their meal.

Unless otherwise stated all recipes are for one person.

PARTRIDGE EGGS WITH SLOES

INGREDIENTS

- 6–8 red partridge eggs (*Alectoris rufa*) or quail (*Coturnix coturnix*) eggs
- 12–16 sloes (*Prunus spinosa*) (optional)
- olive oil
- salt

DID YOU KNOW THAT...?

Many prehistoric archeological sites have revealed a large amount of anthropized egg shells, suggesting that the eggs were eaten by humans.

Several studies have reported partridge hunting in the Middle and Upper Paleolithic Era, as demonstrated by bones found in Spain, in the caves of Carihuela and Las Ventanas (Granada), the Tossal de la Roca (Alicante), and the Cova dels Blaus (Castellón).

MODERN PREPARATION

NB: *partridge eggs are not available all the year around. You can replace them with quail eggs.*

- Firstly, be aware that you cannot shell the eggs of a partridge or quail in the same way as those of a chicken, due to their size and fragility as well as the membrane on the inside. Use a sharp knife to perforate the top part of the shell, and to avoid breaking the yolk do not go in deep. Gradually cut the shell open. The eggs are at their best at room temperature.
- Heat a few drops of oil in a frying pan. When the oil is hot, carefully add the egg (or eggs—their small size allows 2 or more to be fried at once) and cook them until they are ready.
- Add the sloes (double the amount of eggs) for a sweet–sour touch.
- Transfer the eggs to a plate and season with salt.

PALEO-STYLE PRESENTATION

- In springtime, when partridges lay their eggs, our ancestors would search out their nests and gather their eggs. At other times of the year, they would be able to collect other kinds of egg.
- Sloes and partridge eggs do not appear at the same time of year. Sloes keep well and the fruit could have been stored in a cool dry place.
- They would have heated a piece of flat stone over a fire and cooked the eggs on it. Once they were cooked, they could add sloes as an accompaniment.

STONE-FRIED OSTRICH EGG WITH CHIVES

INGREDIENTS

- 1 ostrich (*Struthio camelus*) egg
- chives (*Allium schoenoprasum*), chopped
- olive oil
- pepper
- salt

MODERN PREPARATION

NB: *ostrich eggs can be found in specialist stores. One egg weighs about 3½ lb / 1.5 kg and is therefore sufficient for more than 1 person.*

- Shelling an ostrich egg is a complicated affair. Put it into a container where it cannot move, or hold it firmly with your hand. Make a hole in the top with a small saw, taking care not to break the yolk. An alternative is to use a small hammer to break the shell gradually. Once the shell is removed, you can carefully cut off the membrane.
- Heat plenty of oil in a large frying pan—15–20 inches / 40–50 cm in diameter—and when it is sizzling hot add the egg white and spread it over the pan.
- After 3–4 minutes it will have turned white. At this point you can drop the yolk in the center. Season with salt and pepper and finish cooking the egg.
- Serve in the pan, with the chopped chives sprinkled on top.

PALEO-STYLE PREPARATION

- In springtime, prehistoric people would have searched out an ostrich nest and collected a freshly laid egg.
- The egg would be broken on a heated piece of flat stone over a fire and cooked.
- A garnish of herbs that were available could be added.
- Once the egg was cooked, it would be removed from the fire and eaten directly off the stone.

DID YOU KNOW THAT...?

Ostrich eggs were engraved and used as containers between 8,600 and 6,680 years ago in Hassi-Mouillah, in the Ouargla region of present-day Algeria.

Ostrich eggs contain little cholesterol and are therefore recommended for a healthy diet.

EGGS COOKED ON EMBERS

INGREDIENTS

- quail (*Coturnix coturnix*) eggs
- chicken (*Gallus domesticus*) eggs
- goose (*Anser anser*) eggs
- olive oil (optional)
- pepper (optional)
- salt (optional)

MODERN PREPARATION

NB: *you can use any type of egg for this recipe. Make sure that their weight does not exceed 3½ oz / 100 g.*

– Heat water in a saucepan (sufficient to cover the eggs).

– When the water starts to boil, add the chicken eggs, taking care not to break them.

– Three minutes later, add the goose eggs, and 2 minutes after that the quail eggs, again taking care not to break them. Cook all the eggs for a further 5–6 minutes.

– After a total cooking time of 10–12 minutes, remove the saucepan from the heat. Transfer all the eggs to a bowl containing ice and cold water to stop the cooking process and make it easier to peel the eggs.

– Now peel the eggs. Be extremely careful to keep them intact. Season with salt and pepper. Drizzle with oil.

PALEO-STYLE PREPARATION

– Eggs would be collected from the nests that our ancestors came across in the woods. Those that were fairly small in size would be the most suitable.

– They would make a fire with wood, preferably pine wood, and wait until the embers were glowing.

– The eggs would be placed directly on top. They would cook in 5–15 minutes, depending on the size.

– Then the eggs would be peeled and held in the hands to eat.

DID YOU KNOW THAT…?

Eggs are very rich in protein and minerals, particularly iron, potassium, calcium, phosphorus, and magnesium.

SNAILS COOKED ON EMBERS WITH MINT

INGREDIENTS

- 20 snails (*Helix aspersa*)
- 20 mint leaves (*Mentha spp.*)
  + chopped mint
- olive oil
- pepper
- salt

Snails are endangered animals and some species are not edible. It is forbidden to collect them.

MODERN PREPARATION

NB: *if you buy snails they are ready to cook. When our ancestors gathered them in the countryside, they had to purge them. They would be left in a bag without food for several days to eliminate any impurities.*

- Pre-heat the oven to 350 °F / 180 °C.
- Cover a shallow metal tray with newspaper and place the snails on it, openings up. Sprinkle with a generous amount of salt.
- Put them in the oven for 10–15 minutes.
- After this time, open the oven. Drizzle the snails with oil, sprinkle with chopped mint, season with pepper, and cook for a further 10–15 minutes. Two minutes before switching off the oven, insert a mint leaf into each snail opening.
- Before serving, sample a snail to check whether they are ready. If they are overcooked you will not be able to remove them from their shells.

PALEO-STYLE PREPARATION

- Snails would be much easier to find in the countryside on a rainy day than on a dry one.
- Our ancestors would probably have added extra ingredients to enhance the flavor, and mint leaves would be ideal.
- Those could be rolled up with their fingers so a leaf could be placed in each snail shell.
- A fire—holm-oak wood would be particularly good—would be made and cooking would begin when the embers were glowing.
- The snails would cook in about 15 minutes, depending on the heat generated by the fire.

DID YOU KNOW THAT...?

Eating snails became general around the end of the Pleistocene Era (about 20,000 years ago) and by the early Holocene Era (about 11,600–8,900 years ago) it had become extremely common.

The Paleolithic site with evidence of the oldest recorded consumption of snails in Europe is the Cova de la Barriada in Benidorm, Spain. This dates back some 30,000 years.

STONE-GRIDDLED SNAILS WITH RABBIT

INGREDIENTS

- 1 rabbit (*Oryctolagus cuniculus*) or hare (*Lepus europaeus*)
- 24 snails (*Helix aspersa*)
- rosemary (*Rosmarinus officialis*)
- olive oil
- salt

MODERN PREPARATION

- Cook the snails in the same way as in the previous recipe, replacing mint with rosemary.
- While the snails are cooking, heat a few drops of oil on a griddle and add the rabbit (previously salted).
- Cook for about 20 minutes over low to medium heat and drizzle on a little more oil from time to time to moisten the meat.
- After this, turn up the heat to brown the rabbit on both sides, and then add a little rosemary.
- Serve the rabbit accompanied by the snails.

PALEO-STYLE PREPARATION

- A rabbit or hare would be caught with a lasso or other type of trap.
- The snails would be collected. If it had rained recently they would perhaps have had some stored.
- The rabbit or hare would be skinned and its entrails removed. Then it would be cut it into 2. For this recipe a forequarter would be used.
- The fire would be prepared. Once glowing embers could be seen, a sheet of stone would be put on top and left until it was extremely hot. The rabbit and snails would be placed on it.
- After cooking everything for 35 minutes or so, the meal would be ready to eat.

DID YOU KNOW THAT...?

Rabbit is a very healthy, nutritious food with low fat content. It has been found on many archeological sites, but hominids were not the only ones who ate it. It is the foremost prey of the Iberian lynx, as may be seen in the Doñana National Park in Huelva, Spain.

RAZOR CLAMS
WITH ROSEMARY

INGREDIENTS

- 18 razor clams
  (*Ensis spp.*)
- 1 sprig of rosemary
  (*Rosmarinus officinalis*)
- olive oil
- salt

MODERN PREPARATION

- The day before cooking, cover the razor clams with salted water to remove any sand. Then wash them and dry them with kitchen paper.
- Heat 3½ tablespoons / 50 ml of oil in a frying pan and add some finely chopped rosemary. Allow the herb to impregnate the oil with its aroma. Put aside.
- In the same frying pan, drizzle in a few drops of oil and, once it is hot, add the razor clams.
- Turn the razor clams over when they start to open, to make sure they are thoroughly cooked. This will take about 3–5 minutes.
- Before serving the razor clams, drizzle them with the rosemary oil and garnish with a few more rosemary leaves.

PALEO-STYLE PREPARATION

- At low tide, some razor clams would be collected on the beach.
- Rosemary could be found in the mountains, and chopped very finely for this recipe.
- A fire, preferably made with pine wood, would be made.
- When the embers were glowing, the razor clams would be placed in them for 5 minutes.
- Once the razor clams opened, they would be sprinkled with the rosemary before eating.

DID YOU KNOW THAT...?

Rosemary is highly aromatic and it also has many medicinal properties, including enhancement of the secretion of bile. It is a diuretic and a major antioxidant, as well as being very rich in minerals (potassium, iron, and magnesium) and vitamins (A, B, and C).

BOILED RAZOR CLAMS WITH MINT

INGREDIENTS

- 12 razor clams
  (*Ensis macha*)
- mint (*Mentha*)
- salt

MODERN PREPARATION

- Remember that you must leave the razor clams in salted cold water to remove any sand. Then wash them and dry them with kitchen paper.
- Pour a glass of water into a frying pan or shallow saucepan. Add whole mint leaves and razor clams. Boil the water and cook the razor clams until they open.
- Meanwhile, chop up some more mint leaves.
- Once the razor clams are open, transfer them to a plate, sprinkle with the chopped mint, and garnish with a few whole mint leaves.

PALEO-STYLE PREPARATION

- Our ancestors would collect some razor shells from the beach.
- While walking in the countryside, they could pick some mint leaves. For this recipe a few would be kept whole, and the rest chopped.
- A fire would be prepared and a tripod placed over it.
- A pot of water would be hung from the tripod. The razor clams would be boiled in it for about 10 minutes.
- After this, the chopped mint would be added and boiled for a few seconds to enhance the flavor of the clams.

DID YOU KNOW THAT...?

The archeological site of El Retamar (Puerto Real) in the Bay of Cadiz, Spain, has revealed the human manipulation of mollusks—particularly bivalves such as razor clams—in the Mesolithic Era (i.e., between the end of the Paleolithic Era and the beginning of the Neolithic).

Mint is highly aromatic and also has sedative properties. It is a source of vitamin A, folic acid, calcium, and potassium.

STONE-GRIDDLED CLAMS WITH QUAIL

INGREDIENTS

- 12 top-quality clams
  (*Mercenaria mercenaria*)
- 1 medium-size quail
  (*Coturnix coturnix*) or
  1 partridge (*Alectoris rufa*)
- olive oil
- pepper
- salt

MODERN PREPARATION

- Firstly, leave the clams to soak for an hour in a bowl of salted water to remove any traces of sand. Then rinse them and leave them on kitchen paper to absorb any remaining water.
- Scorch the quail, clean it thoroughly, and season with salt and pepper.
- Brush the quail with olive oil.
- Pour a little oil onto a hot broiler or griddle. Add the quail and lower the heat. Turn it over so that it browns on all sides, drizzling it with a little more oil to stop it from drying.
- Meanwhile, cook the clams in a saucepan with a little water until they open. Drain the clams and put aside, covered.
- When the quail is golden brown, transfer it to a serving plate, drizzle on some oil, and accompany it with a handful of clams.

PALEO-STYLE PREPARATION

- Clams could be gathered on the beach by Paleolithic people.
- They would be wash thoroughly, individually.
- Depending on the season, a quail or partridge would be caught.
- The bird would be scalded, then plucked and cleaned.
- The bird would be cooked on a hot stone for 25 minutes, or until it looked crispy and golden brown.
- Five minutes before the quail was ready, the clams would be added. When they opened, the meal was ready.

DID YOU KNOW THAT...?

Apart from being used as food, mollusks such as clams sometimes served to make jewelry. One example can be found in the Molí del Salt (Vimbodí i Poblet, Tarragona, Spain), which contained the remains of pendants made with shells around 14,000 years ago.

STEAMED CLAMS
WITH CELERY

INGREDIENTS

- 12 clams (*Mercenaria mercenaria*)
- 1 stick of celery (*Apium graveolens*)
- celery powder (optional)
- olive oil
- salt

MODERN PREPARATION

- Leave the clams to soak for an hour in a bowl of salted water to remove any sand. Then rinse and dry them thoroughly.
- Once the clams are clean, heat 2 tablespoons of olive oil in a saucepan. When the oil is hot, add the clams and season with salt. Stir occasionally with a wooden spoon.
- Meanwhile, chop the celery finely. Put aside.
- Once all the clams have opened, sprinkle with the chopped celery (without removing the pan from the heat). Stir with a wooden spoon so that the clams absorb the flavor of the celery. Serve in small bowls.
- If you like strong flavors, you can dust the clams with celery powder just before serving.

PALEO-STYLE PREPARATION

- Clams would be found on the beach by our ancestors.
- They would pick some celery and chop it finely.
- A fire would be built and water would be boiled on it in a leather receptacle. A wooden grill would be placed 1 inch / 5 cm above it, and the claims would be placed on top. They would slowly cook in the steam.
- After 15 minutes, or when the clams had opened, they would be sprinkled with celery.

DID YOU KNOW THAT...?

Celery has many medicinal properties: it is a blood tonic and diuretic, has a sedative effect, and helps combat liver disease.

MUSSELS WITH GRAPES

INGREDIENTS

- 12 mussels (*Mytilus edulis*)
- 1 bunch of grapes (*Vitis vinífera*)
- ½ lemon (*Citrus limon*)
- olive oil
- pepper

MODERN PREPARATION

- Firstly, clean the mussels by pulling off the beards and scraping any barnacles off the shells.
- Put a saucepan over medium heat, pour in some oil, and add the mussels, lemon, and pepper.
- Cover the saucepan and leave to cook for 10 minutes.
- After this time, check that the mussels have opened. Remove them from the heat.
- Shell the mussels and put them in a bowl.
- Serve them accompanied by grapes. You could also serve them in their shells, with a grape in each. Eat the mussel and grape together.

PALEO-STYLE PREPARATION

- Mussels would be gathered from rocks on the sea shore.
- The mussels would be cooked on a stone set on a fire.
- When the mussels opened, a grape could be placed inside each.
- The mussels and the grapes would then be eaten together.

DID YOU KNOW THAT...?

Mussels have high protein content but they need to be eaten in large amounts to obtain optimal energy. It is therefore a mistake to think of them as starters or snacks (as we usually do) rather than a main course.

SMOKED
MUSSELS

INGREDIENTS

- 12 mussels (*Mytilus edulis*)
- Neptune grass (*Posidonia oceanica*) or wakame seaweed
- ¾ cup / 200 ml water
- olive oil
- pepper
- coarse salt

MODERN PREPARATION

NB: *we shall use wakame seaweed as the sale of Neptune grass is prohibited.*

- Firstly, clean the mussels by pulling off the beards and scraping any barnacles off the shells.
- Put the water into a large saucepan, add wakame, and leave the seaweed to hydrate for 2 minutes. Then season with coarse salt and ground pepper, and drizzle on some oil.
- Add the mussels and turn the heat to medium. Once the water has boiled, cook for a further 5–6 minutes. Stir occasionally so that the seaweed flavor penetrates the mussels once they are open.
- After this time, strain off any remaining water and serve the mussels in a bowl.

PALEO-STYLE PREPARATION

- Mussels were gathered from rocks on the sea shore.
- Neptune grass that had been washed onto the beach would be gathered if available.
- A fire would be made using any wood available.
- Once the fire was blazing, the mussels would be added on top of the Neptune grass so that they cooked in its smoke and absorbed its aroma.

DID YOU KNOW THAT...?

Neptune grass grows in spectacular meadows on the seabed. It is extremely fragile and even today little is known about it. What we do know is that human intervention in these meadows (e.g., by bottom trawling) and pollution from toxic residues represent a considerable threat to their survival. Accordingly, the harvesting or sale of Neptune grass is now forbidden.

FRESHWATER CRABS COOKED ON EMBERS WITH THYME

INGREDIENTS

- 6 freshwater crabs
  (*Potamon ibericum*)
- thyme (*Thymus vulgaris*)
- olive oil
- salt

MODERN PREPARATION

NB: *both sea crabs and freshwater crabs can be used for this recipe.*

- Heat a little oil in a frying pan or on a griddle.
- Once the oil is hot, add the crabs and cook them over low heat for 6–7 minutes. Season with a little salt.
- After this, add the thyme and cook for a further 6–7 minutes, covered. Move the frying pan from time to time to ensure that the crabs are cooked on all sides.
- Serve the crabs garnished with a sprig of thyme.

PALEO-STYLE PREPARATION

- Our ancestors would be taught when young how to make a creel (basket) or another type of trap for river crabs. Then they would wait for their prey to come.
- Once they had their crabs, they would light a fire and wait until they saw some glowing embers.
- They would put the crabs on the embers along with the thyme, and cook them for 15 minutes.
- After that, they would remove the crabs from the fire and eat them.

DID YOU KNOW THAT…?

Fossils found in the Daughters of Jacob Bridge (one of the most important archeological sites in Israel, spanning a period stretching from 250,000 to 1.5 million years ago) have produced some very interesting data on the prehistoric diet. The findings included fossils of crabs.

SCRAMBLED PARTRIDGE EGGS WITH CRABS AND ASPARAGUS

INGREDIENTS

- 6 river crabs (*Potamon ibericum*)
- 12 spears of wild asparagus (*Asparagus officianalis*)
- 6 red partridge (*Alectoris rufa*) eggs or quail (*Coturnix coturnix*) eggs
- olive oil
- pepper
- salt

MODERN PREPARATION

NB: *this recipe is better with river crabs.*

- Wash and rinse the asparagus. Cut off the base, 2 inches / 5 cm from the end, and discard.
- Heat salted water in a saucepan. When it reaches boiling point, add the asparagus spears and scald them for 2–3 minutes. Then remove them from the heat, rinse, and put aside.
- Peel the raw crabs, taking care to keep them intact. Put aside.
- Shell the eggs on a plate (see method on page 18). Whisk them lightly and put aside.
- Put a little oil in a frying pan and cook the crabs until they turn bright red. Add the asparagus. Stir with a wooden spoon and add the whisked eggs. Season with salt and pepper. Keep stirring constantly until the eggs have set.
- Transfer everything to a serving plate and eat while still piping hot.

PALEO-STYLE PREPARATION

- In prehistoric times river crabs could be caught in clean water in season (before and during the summer). Asparagus could be found on the edges of footpaths and tracks, and eggs in nests, especially on the ground.
- A fire would be made and a tripod placed over it.
- The crabs were placed in a receptacle, hung from the tripod, and boiled for 15 minutes. After this, the receptacle was removed and a piece of stone was placed on the fire.
- The crabs' exoskeleton was next removed, leaving the soft inner parts.
- The asparagus and eggs were cooked on the stone, and then the crabs were added.
- This meal would be eaten off the stone used to cook it.

DID YOU KNOW THAT...?

Crabs offer great health benefits as they are rich in vitamins and minerals. Do not eat them in excess, however, as this can raise your levels of uric acid.

STONE-GRIDDLED CRABS WITH GARLIC AND BAY LEAVES

INGREDIENTS

- 6 freshwater crabs
  (*Potamon ibericum*)
- bay leaves (*Laurus nobilis*)
  + extra leaves for garnish
- garlic (*Allium sativum*)
- olive oil
- salt

MODERN PREPARATION

- Heat some oil in a frying pan or griddle with a few bay leaves. Allow the bay leaves to release their aroma and then remove them, to prevent them from burning. Put the frying pan or griddle aside.
- Peel and slice the garlic.
- Put the crabs in the frying pan or griddle and cook them over low heat for 6–7 minutes. Add a little salt.
- After this time, cover the pan and cook for a further 6–7 minutes. Keep moving the pan so that the crabs are cooked on all sides.
- One or 2 minutes before the crabs are cooked, add the garlic. Continue cooking until the garlic turns golden.
- Serve the crabs garnished with the garlic and the extra bay leaves.

PALEO-STYLE PREPARATION

- Crabs could be caught in the clean waters of a river in season, before and during the summer.
- Our ancestors would make a fire and place a flat stone on top. It would have been heated until extremely hot.
- The crabs would be placed on the stone and left until they were cooked (about 15 minutes).
- When the crabs were almost done, bay leaves and garlic could be added, so that the crabs absorbed their aroma.

SKEWERED SALMON
WITH FENNEL

INGREDIENTS

- 1 salmon (*Salmo salar*) or 1 salmon fillet
- 5–6 fennel bulbs (*Foeniculum vulgare*), leaves and stalks removed
- olive oil
- pepper
- salt

MODERN PREPARATION

- Remove the salmon skin and roughly cut the flesh into chunks (the larger the pieces, the juicier they will be). Sprinkle with a little oil and season with salt and pepper. Put aside.
- Heat salted water in a saucepan. When it reaches boiling point, add the fennel bulbs and cook for 5–8 minutes (they should not become too soft).
- Pre-heat the oven to 375 °F / 190 °C.
- Once the bulbs are cooked, strain and transfer them to an oven dish. Drizzle with oil and roast for 25–30 minutes. Leave to cool, then cut into pieces of an appropriate size for skewering.
- Prepare the skewers by threading on alternate pieces of salmon and fennel. Continue in this way, and then sprinkle with salt.
- Heat a tablespoon of oil in a frying pan or on a griddle, and then arrange the skewers in the pan so they do not touch each other. Keep the heat low at first, for about 10 minutes, turning the skewers several times so that the fish and fennel cook on all sides. Then briefly raise the heat (for about 2 minutes) to brown the ingredients, without letting the salmon get dry.
- If the salmon does start to become dry, you can cook it for less time and then put the skewer on a plate and cover it with aluminum wrap to allow it to finishing cooking with its own heat.
- Serve the skewers with oil drizzled on top.

DID YOU KNOW THAT...?

Fennel is a plant that grows wild all around the Mediterranean basin owing to the favorable climatic conditions. Its slight aniseed flavor makes it a herb that combines particularly well with fish.

PALEO-STYLE PREPARATION

- Paleolithic people would catch a salmon and gather some fennel.
- They would wash the fennel and clean the salmon.
- Then the fennel and the salmon would be cut into chunks.
- Perhaps they would skewer a chunk of salmon and another of fennel, and so on, successively.
- The skewers could be placed on the embers of a fire made with oak or holm-oak wood and cooked for about 15 minutes.
- They would be eaten directly off the stick.

SMOKED SALMON

INGREDIENTS

- 1 adult salmon (*Salmo salar*) or 1 salmon steak (2 lb / 1 kg)
- dill (*Anethum graveolens*)
- mint (*Mentha*)
- chard (*Beta vulgaris*)
- olive oil
- peppercorns
- 1 package of smoked salt

MODERN PREPARATION

NB: *you will obtain marinated salmon from this recipe, as smoking it at home is hardly a viable proposition. However, the result is practically the same.*

- Debone the salmon. The biggest ones will be easy to remove, but the smaller ones will require patience—and a pair of tweezers.
- Mix the smoked salt and the dill in a large bowl.
- Put the salmon on top of the bed created by this mixture, with the skin facing upward. Cover the top of the salmon with the mixture and then cover the bowl with plastic wrap.
- Put some kind of weight on top of the plastic wrap (such as a soda can or jam jar).
- Leave the bowl in the fridge for 2–3 days.
- Prepare some mint oil: chop the mint leaves, cover them with plenty of olive oil, and leave to marinate.
- Once the salmon has marinated, uncover it, remove it from the mixture, and wash and dry it.
- Cut the fish into very thin fillets.
- Serve the salmon on chard leaves garnished with a few peppercorns, and drizzle with the mint oil.

PALEO-STYLE PREPARATION

- Paleolithic people would obtain an adult salmon from a river with clean water.
- The salmon would be cut into fillets (of the thickness preferred).
- A fire would be made wth bryophytes (mosses) and a tripod put up over it. The fillets would have hung from the tripod.
- Once the salmon was smoked, it would be left for 5–6 days before eating.
- It could be garnished with any herb they had to hand.

DID YOU KNOW THAT...?

Remains of this species of salmon were found on the German site of Geißenklösterle, which dates back between 32,000 and 43,000 years.

Chard is very diuretic and tonifying, and it also enhances the brain and the memory.

TROUT WITH ROSEMARY AND NUTS

INGREDIENTS

- 1 trout (*Salmo trutta*)
- rosemary (*Rosmarinus officinalis*)
- 12 filberts (*Corylus avellana*)
- 24 pine nuts (*Pinus pinea*)
- olive oil
- pepper
- salt

MODERN PREPARATION

- Ask at your fish counter to have your trout cleaned and deboned. Or do it yourself, by removing the trout's central and side bones and opening it out like a book.
- Season the trout with salt and pepper, cover it with rosemary, and close it.
- Put a little oil on a hot non-stick griddle and add the trout, drizzling on a few more drops of oil. Firstly, sauté it over medium heat and then turn up the heat at the last moment to brown the trout slightly.
- Meanwhile, toast the pine nuts and filberts in a frying pan until they are shiny and golden (the frying pan can be dry as these nuts release their own oil). The filberts will start to give off a nutty smell.
- Once the trout is ready, serve it accompanied by the nuts.

PALEO-STYLE PREPARATION

- The traditional method our ancestors used to catch a trout (which is now forbidden in many places) involved putting their hands under a boulder and catching the fish hidden underneath. One of the authors (Eudald Carbonell) is highly skilled in this art.
- A sprig of rosemary would perhaps be picked to go with the trout.
- The trout could be opened out into 2 halves, and then closed after the rosemary had been placed inside.
- A fire, preferably made with hydrophilic wood such as *Populus alba* (black poplar) or *Alnus glutinosa* (alder), would be made and left until some glowing embers could be seen.
- The trout would be put on a sheet of slate or some other flat stone and cooked for 10–15 minutes.
- The fish could be accompanied by pine nuts and filberts.
- For an exotic touch, the fire could be made with some different material, such as palm leaves.

DID YOU KNOW THAT...?

Fossil remains of trout dating back 30,000–43,000 years were found on the Geißenklösterle site in Germany.

The inhabitants of Aitutaki in Polynesia were making fires with palm leaves 3,000 years ago.

BAKED TROUT STUFFED WITH STRAWBERRIES AND ACCOMPANIED BY RED FRUITS

INGREDIENTS

- 1 trout (*Salmo trutta*) weighing about 8 oz / 250 g
- 12 wild strawberries (*Fragaria vesca*)
- 12 raspberries (*Rubus idaeus*)
- 4 madrone (*Arbutus unedo*) berries
- 1 fig (*Ficus carica*)
- 6 sloes (*Prunus spinona*)
- purslane, as garnish
- olive oil
- pepper
- salt

MODERN PREPARATION

- Pre-heat the oven to 400 °F / 200 °C.
- You can buy a trout already cleaned, or clean it yourself by removing its central and side bones and opening it out like a book.
- Season the trout with salt and pepper, cover it with the strawberries, and close.
- Grease an oven dish with oil, add the trout, and drizzle on a little more oil.
- Bake the trout for 10–12 minutes, keeping an eye on it.
- After this time, remove the dish from the oven and serve the trout accompanied by the fig (split into 2), the sloes, the madrone berries, and the raspberries. Finally, add some purslane as a garnish.

PALEO-STYLE PREPARATION

- Trout caught at an altitude of 3,300–6,600 feet / 1,000–2,000 m would be ideal for this recipe.
- While out fishing, our ancestor could pick some raspberries, madrones, sloes, figs, wild strawberries, and purslane.
- The trout would be cleaned and opened out into 2 halves. Wild strawberries could be placed inside it.
- A hole would be dug and a fire would be made in it. Black pine (*Pinus uncinata*) would be ideal for this.
- The trout would be placed between 2 pieces of moss, as if making a sandwich. It would be put on the embers in the oven and covered, then left to cook for 45–60 minutes.
- It could be served by placing it on some fern leaves and holding it in the hands, with red fruits alongside.

DID YOU KNOW THAT...?

Freshwater fish such as trout and salmon are among the animals depicted in the cave paintings in Niaux, Mas d'Azil (France), which date back 12,000–14,000 years.

TROUT
WITH MUSTARD

INGREDIENTS

- 1 river trout (*Salmo trutta*)
- brown mustard (*Brassica juncea*) seeds, or ground mustard
- olive oil
- pepper
- salt

MODERN PREPARATION

NB: *when used on its own, mustard has a very strong flavor, so adjust the amount you add at the end of the cooking process to your taste.*

- A whole trout is used in this recipe. Buy it already cleaned or clean it yourself.
- If you have mustard seeds, grind them in a mortar to obtain fine powder. Put aside.
- Heat a little oil in a non-stick frying pan and add the trout, seasoned with salt and pepper.
- Firstly, cook the trout over low to medium heat so that it is done inside, then turn up the heat at the last moment to brown the fish on both sides.
- Remove the trout from the heat and serve dusted with the mustard.

PALEO-STYLE PREPARATION

- An adult river trout would be caught and cleaned.
- To make the mustard, a sprig of the brown mustard plant would be picked and pounded into powder.
- A fire would be made, and a stone (such as crystallized travertine) would be placed on it. When the stone was hot, the trout would be placed directly on it and cooked for about 15 minutes, turning occasionally.
- Finally, when the trout was ready, the mustard could be sprinkled on top.

DID YOU KNOW THAT...?

Hundreds of fireplaces dating back 40,000–60,000 years were discovered in the Abric Romaní in Capellades (Barcelona, Spain). Some of these contained circular sheets of crystallized travertine that had been heated by fire and were probably used for cooking by induction.

TUNA FISH WITH PINE NUTS COOKED ON EMBERS

INGREDIENTS

- 1 tuna fish (*Thunnus thynnus*) or 1 flank of tuna fish
- 1 pine cone (*Pinus pinea*) or peeled pine nuts
- olive oil
- salt

MODERN PREPARATION

- For this recipe you can buy a whole flank of tuna fish and cut it to your required thickness, or you can ask at your fish counter to have it cut.
- Brown the pine nuts in a frying pan and then put them aside. No oil is required as these nuts release their own.
- Heat a little oil in a non-stick frying pan over high heat. Sprinkle salt on the tuna and when the oil starts to smoke add the fish to the frying pan. Turn it so that both sides are seared. (This method means that the fish is browned on the outside but remains raw inside. You can continue cooking it for longer if you prefer.)
- Remove the frying pan from the heat and cut the fish lengthwise, stopping before you reach the end. Insert the pine nuts and leave the fish for a few more seconds, so that the nuts absorb its flavor through the residual heat of the frying pan.
- Transfer the tuna fish to a serving plate.

PALEO-STYLE PREPARATION

- For this recipe our ancestors would catch or perhaps trade a tuna fish.
- They would forage for a pine cone in mixed woodland or a pine forest. Sometimes they would find a cone on the ground. If not, they would be able to knock a cone off a branch with a stick.
- The pine nuts would be removed and peeled.
- The flank of the tuna fish would be cleaned and cut lengthwise. Then the peeled pine nuts would be inserted.
- The fish would be placed on the embers of a fire and cooked for 15–20 minutes, according to taste.

DID YOU KNOW THAT...?

Our ancestors were skilled fishermen. This can be seen from the remains found in a small cave on the eastern tip of East Timor, which include the bones of over 2,800 fish (including tuna) dating back some 40,000 years.

STONE-GRIDDLED TUNA FISH WITH JUNIPER BERRIES AND ROCKET

INGREDIENTS

- 1 slice of tuna fish (*Thunnus thynnus*), 1–1½ in / 3–4 cm thick
- 12 juniper berries (*Juniperus communis*)
- 4 or 6 rocket leaves (*Eruca sativa*)
- olive oil
- pepper
- salt

MODERN PREPARATION

- Season the tuna fish with salt and pepper.
- Heat some oil in a griddle, over high heat. When the oil starts to smoke, add the tuna. Turn the fish over so that both sides are seared. This means that it is browned on the outside but remains slightly raw on the inside. Add the juniper berries, to allow the fish to absorb their flavor. Drizzle a little more oil on top so that the fish does not dry out.
- Once the tuna fish and juniper berries are browned, remove the griddle from the heat and dice the fish.
- Serve on a bed of rocket leaves.

PALEO-STYLE PREPARATION

- A tuna fish would be bought or traded.
- Juniper berries and a few rocket leaves would be picked in the countryside.
- The fish was cooked for 5 minutes on each side, on a piece of flat stone placed on a fire.
- Once the tuna fish was cooked, it would be served on a bed of rocket leaves and sprinkled with juniper berries.

DID YOU KNOW THAT...?

The first archeological record of the consumption of tuna fish was found on a 9,200-year-old wall painting in the Genovés Cave on the island of Levanzo, near Sicily (Italy).

PHEASANT WITH CHESTNUTS

INGREDIENTS

- 1 pheasant (*Phasianus colchicus*)
- 12 chestnuts (*Castanea sativa*)
- lard
- olive oil
- pepper
- salt

MODERN PREPARATION

- Firstly, roast the chestnuts. Pre-heat the oven to 350 °F / 180 °C. Meanwhile, make a cross-shape incision in the top of each chestnut with a knife (this makes them easier to peel). Put them in an oven dish and roast for 15 minutes. After this time, turn them over and leave for a further 15 minutes. (They are ready when they open.) Take the chestnuts out of the oven (without turning it off). Leave to cool, and then peel and chop them.
- While the chestnuts are in the oven, scald, clean, and dry the pheasant.
- Stuff the pheasant with the chopped chestnuts and close its inner cavity with toothpicks. Daub it with lard and season with salt and pepper.
- Place the pheasant on the same oven dish and roast it for 40 minutes. You can then brown it a little in the oven broiler (grill). If it looks dry, drizzle on a little oil.
- Finally, transfer the meat to a plate and serve it whole.

PALEO-STYLE PREPARATION

- The Paleolithic hunter would search for a pheasant or a Eurasian woodcock. It would be scalded, plucked, and cleaned.
- A handful of chestnuts would be peeled and mashed into powder.
- The chestnut powder would be mixed with water to obtain a paste to put inside the bird.
- To cook, a hole would be dug in the ground and a fire started inside it. The bird would be placed inside when the embers were glowing, and cooked for 45–60 minutes. The top of the oven would be covered to improve the cooking process.
- After this, the bird would be eaten, using the hands.

DID YOU KNOW THAT...?

Remains of pheasants dating back to the Magdalenian period (12,000–14,500 years ago) have been found in the Santimamiñe Caves in the Spanish Basque country.

PIGEON STUFFED WITH RED FRUITS

INGREDIENTS

- 1 wild pigeon (*Columba livia*) or 1 partridge (*Perdix perdix*)
- 12 raspberries (*Rubus occidentalis*)
- 12 madrone berries (*Arbutus unedo*)
- 12 blackberries (*Morus nigra*)
- 12 sloes (*Prunus spinosa*)
- lard
- olive oil
- pepper
- salt

MODERN PREPARATION

NB: *a wild pigeon may be hard to find but you can always replace it with a partridge.*

- Wash and dry all the red fruit.
- Scald, wash, and dry the bird. Season it with salt and pepper, both inside and out.
- Pre-heat the oven to 350 °F / 180 °C.
- Daub the bird with lard and sear it in a frying pan over high heat so that it browns on the outside. Remove it from the heat and stuff it with the red fruit. Close the bird's cavity with toothpicks to prevent the stuffing from spilling out.
- Put the bird in an oven dish and roast it for 40 minutes. If it looks dry, drizzle on a little oil.
- Finally, transfer the bird to a plate and serve it whole (having removed the toothpicks, to allow some fruit to fall out and provide a splash of color).

PALEO-STYLE PREPARATION

- The hunter would need first to catch a pigeon. While hunting, they could pick some red fruit.
- The pigeon would be scalded, plucked, and cleaned. It would be stuffed with the red fruit.
- A fire would be made with wood that would burn at a high temperature. The fire would be allowed to go out and then the pigeon would be buried in the ashes.
- Another fire would be lit on top.
- The pigeon would be left to cook for 1 hour, after which the second fire would be allowed to go out. Then the pigeon would be removed and eaten straight away.

DID YOU KNOW THAT...?

The Neanderthals introduced pigeon into their diet between 28,000 and 67,000 years ago. Their remains were found in the Gorham Cave in Gibraltar, Spain, with signs of incisions and burning, indicating that they had been dismembered and cooked.

GUINEA-FOWL WITH GARLIC

INGREDIENTS

- 1 guinea-fowl
  (*Guttera pucherani*)
- 12 cloves of rosy garlic
  (*Allium roseum*) or wild
  garlic
- lard
- olive oil
- pepper
- salt

MODERN PREPARATION

- Scald, wash, and dry the guinea-fowl. Season it with salt and pepper, inside and out.
- Prepare the garlic: use a whole head and also a few loose cloves, all unpeeled.
- Pre-heat the oven to 350 °F / 180 °C.
- Place the guinea-fowl in an oven dish and daub it with lard.
- Roast the bird for 40–50 minutes. Halfway through, add the garlic and sprinkle with a little oil to stop the ingredients from drying.

PALEO-STYLE PREPARATION

- Our ancestors would need to hunt a guinea-fowl and gather some garlic.
- First they would scald and pluck the bird, and then remove the giblets.
- They would then insert the garlic in the bird's cavity.
- A fire would be made, ideally with very dry birch wood (*Betula*), and a stone griddle would be placed on it. The guinea-fowl would be placed on top and cooked for about 40–65 minutes. It would be turned regularly so that it was browned on all sides.

DID YOU KNOW THAT...?

Guinea-fowl is prized for the delicate texture of its tender, succulent meat, and low fat content. It has an abundance of vitamins, proteins, and minerals.

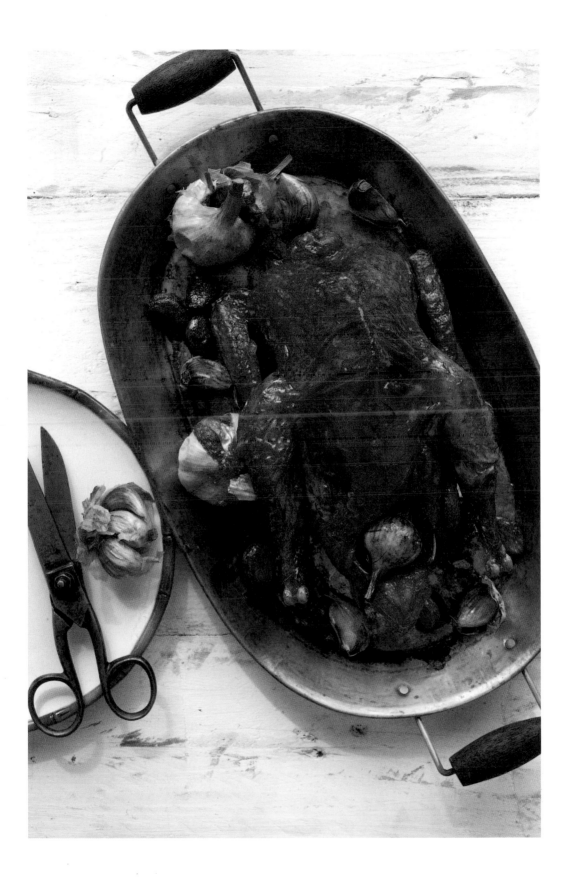

GOOSE WITH OLIVES

INGREDIENTS

- 1 leg of goose (*Anser anser*) or green-necked duck (*Anas platyrhynchos*)
- 6 pitted olives (*Olea europea sativa*)
- 3–4 carrots (*Daucus carota*) (optional)
- 1 tsp thyme (*Thymus vulgaris*) + 1 sprig as garnish
- lard
- olive oil
- pepper
- salt

MODERN PREPARATION

NB: *a goose can normally only be ordered at the beginning of December, before Christmas. Duck is an ideal alternative for this recipe.*

- Pre-heat the oven to 425 °F / 220 °C.
- Wash the leg and season it with salt and pepper to taste. Sprinkle with the thyme and daub the meat with lard.
- Put the meat in an oven dish with a little water and roast it for 30–35 minutes.
- After this time, turn it over and roast for a further 35–40 minutes, so that it is cooked on all sides. If the meat looks dry, sprinkle it with water.
- Meanwhile, add a little oil to a frying pan and sauté the olives and carrots (if used). Put aside. When the bird is almost cooked, add the olives and carrots so that they will absorb its flavor.
- Finally, remove the meat from the oven and serve it accompanied by the olives and carrots. You can garnish the dish with a sprig of thyme.

PALEO-STYLE PREPARATION

- A goose or some other suitable bird would be hunted or traded. It would then be scalded and cleaned, and cut into chunks.
- A handful of olives would be picked.
- An oven would be dug in the ground, and some wood such as alder (*Alnus glutinosa*) would be placed inside and a fire lit. It would be left to burn until some glowing embers could be seen.
- The goose leg and the olives would be wrapped in plant material and put on a flat stone such as a sheet of schist.
- The stone was placed on the embers and covered, and the bird was cooked for about an hour.
- After this time, the oven was uncovered and the meat cut into fillets. Pitted olives were mixed with the meat before it was eaten.

DID YOU KNOW THAT...?

Paintings of geese dating back 12,000–14,000 years were found in the Labastide Cave in France.

RABBIT
WITH HERBS

INGREDIENTS

- ½ rabbit (*Oryctolagus cuniculus*) cut into 10 pieces
- rosemary (*Rosmarinus officinalis*), ground + 2 sprigs
- olive oil
- pepper
- salt

DID YOU KNOW THAT...?

The consumption of rabbit meat has been detected in sites from the Upper Paleolithic Era dating back over 400,000 years. On some sites, such as those of the Molí del Salt and Vimbodí i Poblet, both in Tarragona, Spain, it was the most widely eaten animal around 13,000 years ago, as is evident from the numerous burnt rabbit fossils.

MODERN PREPARATION

- Season the rabbit with salt and pepper, and dust it with the ground rosemary.
- Pre-heat the oven to 350 °F / 180 °C.
- Put 4 tablespoons of oil in a frying pan and fry the rabbit on all sides over high heat.
- Transfer it to an oven dish (complete with the oil) and roast it for 45 minutes. Add the sprigs of rosemary 5 minutes from the end. If the meat looks dry, moisten it with a little oil or a few drops of water.
- Once the meat is cooked, remove it from the oven and transfer it to a serving plate.

PALEO-STYLE PREPARATION

- Our ancestors would have been used to catching a rabbit. It would be skinned and washed, and cut into 2. Each half would be cut into 10 pieces.
- A hole measuring about 15 x 15 x 20 in / 40 x 40 x 50 cm would be dug in soft ground. The hole would be filled with wood (preferably oak, holm oak, or olive) and a fire started with it.
- The rabbit pieces would be placed between rosemary leaves, as for sandwiches, inside a concave stone receptacle. About 1¼ cups / 330 ml of water would be added, and then the receptacle would be covered with a concave stone.
- Once the wood had finished burning, the stone dish would be placed in the hot embers and the hole covered with a clod of earth. The meat would be uncovered from time to time to check its progress and color. It would take 3 hours or more, depending on how well done it was wanted. When the meat was ready, the stone dish would be removed with great care as it would be extremely hot. (Our ancestors perhaps protected their hands with skins.)
- The rabbit would be eaten using the hands.

SKEWERED GOAT

INGREDIENTS

- 7 oz / 200 g goat (*Capra aegagrus hircus*) or kid (leg)
- rosemary (*Rosmarinus officinalis*), ground + sprigs (as garnish)
- olive oil
- pepper
- salt

MODERN PREPARATION

- Chop the leg meat into 6–8 chunks.
- Season these pieces of meat with salt, pepper, and ground rosemary, and then thread them on a skewer.
- Put the skewers on a hot griddle, drizzle them with oil, and cook the meat until it is golden brown. Keep turning the skewers so that they are cooked on both sides, but do not leave them too long in the heat, otherwise they will become dry.
- Finally, transfer the skewers to a plate and serve them garnished with a few sprigs of rosemary.

PALEO-STYLE PREPARATION

- A wild goat that had been hunted would be chopped into chunks.
- Pieces of meat would then be threaded onto a stick.
- The stick was placed directly on the embers of a fire made with oak or holm-oak wood and left to cook for about 15 minutes.
- Our ancestors would have eaten the meat straight off the stick.

DID YOU KNOW THAT...?

The discovery of the tips of projectiles on an archeological site indicates hunting activity, while a close study of the marks made by incisions reveals how particular animals were handled (skinning, boning, etc.).

GRILLED RACK OF GOAT

INGREDIENTS

- rack of 1 young goat
  (*Capra aegagrus hircus*) or
  5–6 ribs of kid
- 12 wild strawberries
  (*Fragaria vesca*)
- 1 bunch rocket leaves
  (*Eruca sativa*)
- olive oil
- pepper
- salt

MODERN PREPARATION

- You can buy a whole rack of goat or individual ribs. Season the meat with salt and pepper.
- Heat a grill greased with oil. Once it is hot, add the goat meat and grill for 2–3 minutes on each side. Bear in mind that ribs are thin and will be very dry if they are overcooked.
- When the meat is done, transfer it to a serving plate and garnish with the wild strawberries and rocket leaves.

PALEO-STYLE PREPARATION

- A wild goat would be hunted and a rack or individual ribs would be prepared.
- A fire would be made, preferably with oak wood, and the meat would be placed directly onto the embers.
- The meat would be griddled for 5 minutes on each side and then eaten with the hands.
- Our ancestors may well have accompanied the meat with wild fruit and green leaves.

DID YOU KNOW THAT...?

We have little information about the prehistoric use of fuel. Most of what is available concerns wood, which can be identified by analyzing the carbon remains found on archeological sites.

STONE-GRIDDLED BEEFSTEAK

INGREDIENTS

- 1 good-quality entrecote of veal or beef (*Bos primigenius taurus*)
- olive oil
- pepper
- beet salt

MODERN PREPARATION

- You can buy beet salt or make it yourself. To do this, take a bagful of grated beets and mix it thoroughly with a generous handful of sea salt flakes, so that the salt soaks up the juice of the beets. Then put the mixture on a tray covered with kitchen paper and leave it in a dry, sunny place where it will dry out completely. Store the beet salt in an airtight container.
- If the steak is fairly thick, decide beforehand how well done you require it.
- Put the griddle over the highest heat possible, drizzle on a few drops of oil, and sear it on one side for about 2 minutes, and then, if the steak is thick, on the other side. With this searing technique, the meat is crispy on the outside and succulent inside.
- If you want the meat well done, put it on a very hot griddle in the same way, but once you have seared it lower the temperature to medium and continue cooking, so that it is done inside.
- In either case, once the steak is cooked transfer it to a plate and season it with the beet salt. This not only enhances its flavor but also adds a pleasing visual touch.

PALEO-STYLE PREPARATION

- A tender joint of beef from any part of the body would be cut into fillets.
- A piece of flat stone such as schist was heated on a fire (preferably made with oak or holm oak).
- Once the stone was piping hot, the meat was placed on top of it. It would be turned for 10 minutes until it was browned on the outside and red inside.
- The meat was probably eaten using a sharpened stick and a flint knife.

DID YOU KNOW THAT...?

Cattle evolved in Africa alongside our hominid ancestors and formed part of their diet right from the start. The two also both began to disperse at around the same time, when the Acheulean culture conquered first North Africa and then Eurasia, 700,000–800,000 years ago.

SMOKED STRIPS OF WILD BOAR WITH SNAP PEAS

INGREDIENTS

- 1 wild boar (*Sus scrofa*) or rashers of smoked bacon
- 12 pods sugar snap peas (*Pisum arvenis*)
- olive oil
- salt

MODERN PREPARATION

NB: *as it is difficult to obtain this recipe's main ingredient and, furthermore, smoke it in a modern domestic setting, it has been replaced by smoked bacon. The result is similar to the original, and very tasty.*

- Wash and dry the sugar snap peas.
- Heat a little oil in a frying pan and fry the rashers of bacon. Once they have browned, remove them from the pan and put them aside.
- Using the same frying pan, and the fat released by the bacon, sauté the sugar snap peas for 5 minutes, covered. You can reduce this cooking time if you scald them beforehand in salted boiling water for 2 minutes.
- Transfer the peas to a serving plate and add the bacon rashers, along with a pinch of salt.

PALEO-STYLE PREPARATION

- Paleolithic people would skin and dismember the wild boar.
- Using its softest parts, they would cut long, thin strips weighing about 1 ounce / 30 g.
- A roughly rectangular fire would be made. It would be covered with bryophytes (mosses and liverworts) to create more smoke.
- The strips of meat would be placed on a piece of wood positioned horizontally 15 inches / 40 cm above the fire.
- The meat would be ready after 2–3 hours.
- Sugar snap peas would be a good accompaniment.

DID YOU KNOW THAT...?

Wild boars have been hunted for food for a very long time, as indicated by their frequent appearance in prehistoric cave paintings.

GRIDDLED WILD BOAR WITH APPLE COMPOTE

INGREDIENTS

- 1 loin of wild boar (*Sus scrofa*) or 1 sirloin steak
- olive oil
- Jamaican chili pepper
- ground pepper
- salt

FOR THE APPLE COMPOTE

- 1 apple (*Malus domestica*)
- 2 tbsp / 30 ml water or apple juice (with no added sugar)

MODERN PREPARATION

NB: *wild boar may be hard to find in your area but you can use pork tenderloin as a substitute.*

- Start making the compote by heating the water or apple juice over medium heat. Peel the apple, cut it into 4, remove the seeds, and chop it into ½ inch / 1 cm cubes. Once the water has boiled, add the apple, stir until the water starts to boil again, then lower the heat and cook the apple for 20 minutes, covered. Stir from time to time. You will see that the apple gets softer and starts to break up, before becoming transparent. Continue stirring with a spoon or fork until you achieve the desired texture (a smooth purée, or still with some pieces of apple). Remove from the heat and put aside.
- Cut the meat into thin strips, no more than ½ in / 1 cm thick, and season with salt and pepper.
- Drizzle a little oil on a griddle, add the strips of meat, and cook them on both sides.
- Transfer to a serving plate. Add the apple compote and a few Jamaican peppers.

PALEO-STYLE PREPARATION

- Our ancestors would need a loin from a hunted wild boar and would cut it into thin fillets ½ inch / 1 cm thick.
- They could pick an apple and dice it with a flint knife.
- The meat would be placed on a hot sheet of stone such as travertine and cooked on both sides for 10 minutes.
- It would be eaten, with the diced apple, off the stone with the help of a sharp stick and a flint knife.

DID YOU KNOW THAT...?

In the seasonal camps established on the banks of the River Freser, a tributary of the River Ter in Girona, Spain, one of the main items on the menu of the hominids who spent their summers on the mountain slopes of Sota Palou in Campdevànol was wild boar, which thrives in dense woodland. The remains on this site date back around 9,000 years.

ROAST WILD BOAR
WITH RED FRUIT SAUCE

INGREDIENTS

- 1 wild boar (*Sus scrofa*) or 1 leg of wild boar
- 1 carrot (*Daucus carota*)
- 1 onion (*Allium cepa*)
- 2 cloves garlic (*Allium sativum*)
- rosemary sprigs (*Rosmarinus officinalis*) (as garnish)
- olive oil or lard
- pepper
- salt
- beet salt

FOR THE RED FRUIT SAUCE

- 2½ cups / 200 g red fruits
- 3 tbsp / 40 ml water

MODERN PREPARATION:

NB: *if you want to prepare the beet salt yourself, see page 74.*

- Daub the leg of wild boar with oil (or lard), season with salt and pepper, and leave to marinate in the fridge for 24 hours. This will soften the meat.
- Pre-heat the oven to 300 °F / 150 °C. Roughly chop the vegetables.
- Put the meat in an oven dish with the juices from the marinade and add the vegetables.
- Roast the meat for 2½ hours. Sprinkle it with water from time to time to stop it dehydrating.
- To make the red fruit sauce, heat the water. When it starts to boil add the fruit. Cook until the fruit is very soft. You can then liquidize the mixture if you want a thin sauce, or you can strain it, pressing with a fork to extract the juice and adding a few pieces of fruit to the sauce.
- Once the wild boar is cooked, carve it into pieces. Pour the sauce on top and garnish with some sprigs of rosemary and beet salt.

PALEO-STYLE PREPARATION

- In the woods a wild boar, preferably an adult, would be hunted.
- If the hunter found some red fruits on the way, they could pick a generous amount to go with the meat.
- The boar would be cleaned and dismembered.
- Our ancestors would dig out an oven measuring 15 x 15 x 20 in / 40 x 40 x 50 cm and make a fire inside with slow-burning calorific wood such as olive, oak, or holm oak.
- The meat was placed directly onto the embers and covered with a handful of herbs, including rosemary.
- The oven was covered with a clod of earth to slow down the combustion and the meat was cooked for 5–6 hours.
- The dish could be served with crushed red fruits and a few sprigs of rosemary.

DID YOU KNOW THAT...?

Wild boar meat is very rich in vitamins, especially vitamin B3, which can help to reduce cholesterol. It is a good alternative to the common pig as it couples a higher quantity of protein with a lower fat content.

WILD BOAR STEW WITH BAY LEAVES AND CHESTNUTS

INGREDIENTS

- 1 wild boar (*Sus scrofa*) or 1 leg or back of wild boar
- 1 stick of celery (*Apium graveolens*)
- 6 chestnuts (*Castanea sativa*)
- bay leaves (*Laurus nobilis*)
- 4 cups / 1 liter water
- olive oil or lard
- pepper
- salt

MODERN PREPARATION

– Cut the wild boar meat into small chunks. To soften the meat, marinade it by daubing it with oil (or lard), seasoning it with salt and pepper, and leaving it in the fridge for 24 hours.

– Wash the stick of celery and cut it into slices.

– Peel the chestnuts and chop them roughly.

– Once the meat has been marinated, brown it with the oil and the juices from the marinade in a saucepan and then add the celery and chestnuts. Sauté all these ingredients for a few minutes and add 2 glasses of water and the bay leaves.

– Cover the saucepan and leave the stew to simmer over low heat. Stir from time to time, adding more water if the liquid starts to evaporate. Cook for about 90 minutes (you can check the progress of the meat by piercing it with a toothpick).

– After this time, turn off the heat and leave the stew to stand for at least 10 minutes.

– Serve in individual bowls.

PALEO-STYLE PREPARATION

– Early man would go to the woods to hunt a wild boar. He would cut it into pieces, including both bones and flesh.

– The meat would be placed inside a skin, along with water and bay leaves.

– The skin was hung from a tripod over a fire. Soon the water would boil.

– Cooking took about 1½ hours. The water would be replenished during the process to prevent the meat from drying out.

– The meat could be accompanied by chestnuts.

DID YOU KNOW THAT...?

Bay leaves enhance the digestive process and relieve stomach aches. They also add a sweet and spicy touch to a dish.

VENISON STEAK WITH GREEN BEANS AND CARROTS

INGREDIENTS

- 1 deer (*Cervus elaphus*) or ¼ loin or tenderloin of a deer or pig
- 1½ cups / 200 g green beans, roughly chopped (*Phaseolus vulgaris*)
- 1 purple carrot (*Daucus carota*)
- olive oil
- pepper
- salt

DID YOU KNOW THAT…?

Remains of deer have often been found on sites dating from the Middle and Upper Pleistocene Era. This has happened, for example, on Spanish sites from the recent Paleolithic period such as the Abric Romaní (Capellades, Barcelona, Spain) and the upper levels of the Gran Dolina de Atapuerca (Burgos, Spain).

MODERN PREPARATION

NB: *venison may be difficult to find if deer are not hunted in your area. You can replace it with pork tenderloin. You may add romesco sauce if you wish.*

- Daub the meat with oil, season it with salt and pepper, and leave it to marinade in the fridge for 24 hours.
- Wash the chopped green beans. Heat some salted water, when it starts to boil add the green beans. Cook them for 15 minutes, then drain and put aside.
- Peel the carrot and slice it thinly. Fry it in hot oil for 10 minutes. Once the carrot is cooked, remove from the pan and put aside on a piece of kitchen paper, to remove any excess oil.
- Heat a griddle over high heat and then add the meat, along with the juices from the marinade. As the meat is quite thick, you must decide beforehand how well you want it done. For rare meat, sear it for 1 minute on each side. For well-done meat, after this initial searing reduce the heat to medium and continue cooking until it is done on the inside.
- Transfer the meat to a serving plate and add the green beans and carrot.
- If you want to complement the dish with a sauce, romesco (based on red pepper and nuts) would be ideal, but this is optional.

PALEO-STYLE PREPARATION

- A deer would be hunted, and a loin cut from it. Wild products such as green beans and bay leaves would be picked to go with it.
- The meat would be placed in a leather receptacle filled with water containing the bay leaves, and boiled gently for 15 minutes.
- After this time, the meat would be removed from the leather bag and placed on the embers of the fire to continue cooking.
- The green beans would be cooked for 15 minutes in the leather bag.
- The meat could be filleted on a piece of stone and the green beans placed on top.
- A stone knife would be used to cut the meat.

HAMBURGER WITH FALSE KETCHUP, MUSTARD, AND ONION

INGREDIENTS

- beef (*Bos primigenius taurus*), ground for modern version—1 cup / 150 g per hamburger
- 2 eggs
- rocket leaves (*Eruca sativa*)
- olive oil
- pepper
- salt

FOR THE FALSE KETCHUP

- 2 cups / 200 g red fruits
- 2½ tbsp / 40 ml water

FOR THE FALSE MUSTARD

- mustard powder or seeds
- water

FOR THE FALSE ONION

- 1 pear (*Pyrus communis*)

DID YOU KNOW THAT...?

Horses were one of the most widely hunted species of the Pleistocene period. They formed an essential part of the meat intake of our prehistoric ancestors, along with deer and bovine animals.

MODERN PREPARATION

- *To make the false ketchup:* heat the water. When it starts to boil, add the fruit and cook until it softens. Liquidize this mixture to obtain a thin sauce and put aside.
- *To make the false mustard:* mix the mustard and water in a blender to obtain a smooth paste. (This will have a strong taste, so do not use too much mustard.) Put aside.
- *To make the false onion:* wash the pear, cut it in 4 and remove the seeds. Slice it thinly. (As pear flesh goes brown very quickly when exposed to the air, leave its preparation until the last moment.)
- Grind the meat and mix it in a bowl with the eggs, salt, and pepper. Make a few balls and squash them so that they are ½–1 inch / 1–2 cm thick, depending on your taste.
- Put a few drops of oil on a griddle and cook the hamburgers over high heat for about 2 minutes. If you prefer the meat well done, continue cooking over lower heat.
- Finally, prepare the serving plate: put a hamburger in place and then put some pear slices on top of it. Put another hamburger on top, and then add some more pear slices. Accompany the dish with the mustard, ketchup, and rocket leaves.

PALEO-STYLE PREPARATION

- Meat would be obtained; horse meat could have been used.
- A pear, some red fruits, and some rocket leaves would be needed, along with some mustard seeds.
- The meat would be sliced thinly and then cut into pieces (as small as possible). It would be crushed to form a compact mass, then shaped with the hands to make flattened ball shapes.
- A fire would be made. When the embers started to glow, a stone would be placed directly on top and the hamburgers would be cooked on it.
- Meanwhile, the red fruit was beaten with water to obtain a purée, and the mustard seeds were ground in a little water.
- When the meat was cooked, the pear slices were placed between 2 hamburgers and then topped with the red fruit purée and the mustard sauce.

BEEF STEW WITH WALNUTS AND APPLE

INGREDIENTS

- beef (*Bos primigenius taurus*)
- 2 apples (*Malus sylvestris*)
- 10 walnuts (*Juglans regia*)
- celery (*Apium graveolens*)
- lard
- pepper
- salt

MODERN PREPARATION

- Roughly cut the meat into chunks and season with salt and pepper. Wash and thinly slice the celery.
- Put the lard and meat in an earthenware casserole over high heat. Brown the meat for about 2 minutes, stirring constantly.
- Add the celery and continue stirring until it also starts to brown. Add sufficient water to cover the ingredients.
- When the water starts to boil, lower the heat to medium. Cover the casserole and cook for about 75 minutes.
- Add the walnuts and apples (chopped and deseeded but unpeeled). Add more salt if required. Cook for a further 15 minutes.
- Before serving, remove from the heat and leave to stand for a short time.

PALEO-STYLE PREPARATION

- Paleolithic people would remove the cheek, whole, from the animal's head.
- They would cut an apple into pieces and shell some walnuts.
- A fire would be made with wild pine wood (*Pinus sylvestris*) and a stone placed on top of it.
- Once the stone was hot, the apple would be placed inside the meat, and together they would be cooked for at least 1½ hours.
- The meat could be accompanied by a few walnuts.

DID YOU KNOW THAT...?

On the Upper Paleolithic French site of Le Solutre, dating back 18,000 years, animal bones give a great deal of information about the diet of prehistoric settlers.

BEEF STEAK WITH WILD STRAWBERRIES

INGREDIENTS

- 1 beef steak (*Bos primigenius taurus*) for each person
- 12 wild strawberries (*Fragaria vesca*)
- olive oil
- pepper
- salt

MODERN PREPARATION

– You can buy individual steaks or, if you have a sirloin available, you can carve them off yourself.
– Wash the strawberries and put aside.
– Drizzle a few drops of oil into a heavy-bottom frying pan. When the oil is hot, add the steak and sear it for 2 minutes on each side. (You can then cook it for more time, if you so desire.)
– Finally, transfer the meat to a serving plate, add salt, and serve it accompanied by a few strawberries.

PALEO-STYLE PREPARATION

– A good piece of meat would be cut from any part of the body, and filleted.
– Our ancestors would perhaps pick a few wild strawberries to eat with their meal.
– They would make a fire, preferably with oak or holm-oak wood, and put a piece of flat stone on top of it.
– Once the stone was hot, the meat was placed on it and cooked for 3–4 minutes on each side.
– The steak could be garnished with strawberries.

DID YOU KNOW THAT...?

Many animal bones have been found on one extremely old and very important archeological site in Spain: the Cau del Duc in Torroella de Montgrí, Girona, Spain, by the mouth of the River Ter.

BEEF
COOKED ON EMBERS

INGREDIENTS

- 1 beef sirloin
- olive oil
- salt
- romesco sauce (optional)

MODERN PREPARATION

NB: *romesco sauce, based on red pepper and nuts, is an ideal accompaniment to meat dishes, but many of its ingredients were unavailable during the Paleolithic period. We suggest it as an optional complement, to respect the realities of those times.*

- Slice the sirloin into fillets ¼–1 inch / 2–3 cm thick. Season with salt and pepper, sprinkle with oil, and leave in the fridge for 1 hour.
- After this time, leave the meat at room temperature before cooking it.
- Before cooking the meat, decide how well done you require it: if you want it rare, put the griddle over maximum heat, sprinkle with a few drops of oil, and sear the meat on one side for 2 minutes and then (depending on the thickness) on the other. Searing the meat in this way leaves the meat juicy on the inside and crispy on the outside. If you want your steak well done, follow the same procedure, but once the meat has been seared, lower the heat to medium and continue cooking until the steak is also done on the inside.
- Once the meat is cooked to your taste, transfer it to a plate and add salt. Eat it on its own or accompanied by romesco sauce.

PALEO-STYLE PREPARATION

- A suitable animal was obtained by hunting, or perhaps found after being killed accidentally.
- Paleolithic people would dismember it and select a front or back limb. The meat would be roughly chopped.
- A fire would be made with wood gathered nearby, and left until glowing embers could be seen.
- The pieces of meat were placed directly onto the embers and cooked until they were ready to eat.

DID YOU KNOW THAT...?

In Australia, where prehistory is considered to have lasted until the 18th century, this recipe could have been used with kangaroo meat. Many aboriginal groups in the central desert and other parts of Australia ate kangaroo until recently, and even now its distinctive flavor is very much appreciated.

ANTELOPE COOKED ON EMBERS WITH CHESTNUTS

INGREDIENTS

- 1 rack of antelope (*Antilope cervicapra*) or 1 loin of deer
- 6 chestnuts (*Castanea sativa*)
- 1 pomegranate (*Punica granatum*)
- olive oil
- pepper
- salt

DID YOU KNOW THAT...?

We know that in the last Ice Age the southeastern parts of the South African savanna were populated by the bluebuck (Hippotragus leucophaeus). This is now extinct, and its disappearance may be partly due to hunting. Its remains have been found in the Wonderwerk Cave in South Africa, which is also the site of one the first recorded barbecues.

MODERN PREPARATION

NB: *as antelope is difficult to find, you can replace it with loin of deer.*

- Chop the meat into cubes measuring 1½–2 inches / 3–4 cm and leave to marinate in the fridge with salt, pepper, and olive oil for 1 hour.
- Meanwhile, roast the chestnuts. Pre-heat the oven to 400 °F / 200 °C. Wash the chestnuts thoroughly and make a cross-shape incision on 1 side (this will make them easier to peel afterward). Put the chestnuts in an oven dish lined with aluminum foil or wax paper and sprinkle them with a little water. Roast them in the middle of the oven for 20 minutes, or until they are soft when pricked. Put aside, wrapped in a dish towel so that they stay hot.
- Remove the seeds of the pomegranate and put aside.
- Once the meat is marinated, heat a griddle over high heat and then add the meat, along with the juices of the marinade. As the meat is quite thick, you must decide how well done you want it. Two minutes of cooking on each side will give you rare meat. If you want it well done, turn down the heat and cook it some more.
- Finally, transfer the meat to a serving plate, accompanied by the roasted chestnuts (still in their skins) and sprinkle the pomegranate seeds on top.

PALEO-STYLE PREPARATION

- An antelope would be hunted and killed, and its rack would be cut out.
- A fire was made, preferably with acacia wood (*Acacia tortilis*), which would have been common in the African savanna.
- The rack of meat would be placed on the fire and cooked to taste.
- Prehistoric people could accompany the meat with pomegranate or chestnuts (either raw or cooked in the same fire).

ROAST REINDEER WITH GARLIC AND THYME

INGREDIENTS

- hindquarters of 1 reindeer (*Rangifer tarandus*) or 1 leg of kid
- thyme (*Thymus vulgaris*)
- 1–2 heads garlic (*Allium sativum*)
- olive oil
- pepper
- salt

MODERN PREPARATION

- Cut the meat into 3 pieces. Season these with salt and pepper and brush them with oil.
- Pre-heat the oven to 400 °F / 200 °C while you prepare the meat.
- Place the meat in an oven dish with the garlic and thyme. Add 1 tablespoon of oil and a little water.
- Put the meat in the oven and roast it for 1 hour.
- After this time, turn the meat over and roast it for a further 40 minutes. Before removing it from the oven, brown it for 1–2 minutes using the oven broiler (grill).
- It is important for the oven dish always to have a little water in it. If it dries up, add some more.
- Serve the meat garnished with the garlic and thyme.

PALEO-STYLE PREPARATION

- The hindquarters of a hunted reindeer were needed for this recipe.
- It was skinned, and then incisions were made with a stone knife along and across its back legs, right down to the bone.
- Wild garlic and some sprigs of thyme were picked.
- When the meat was ready for cooking, an oven was made by digging a hole in the ground. A fire of pine or fir wood was made inside it.
- The reindeer meat was placed inside the hole, between 2 layers of moss, and then buried.
- The meat was roasted for 3–4 hours.

DID YOU KNOW THAT...?

The reindeer was one of the large prehistoric mammals that thrived in a cold climate, along with the wooly mammoth and wooly rhinoceros.

REINDEER COOKED ON EMBERS WITH CHANTERELLES

INGREDIENTS

- forequarters or hindquarters of 1 reindeer (*Rangifer tarandus*) or 1 leg of kid
- 12 chanterelles (*Cantharellus cibarius*)
- olive oil
- pepper
- salt

MODERN PREPARATION

- Cut the meat into fillets 1–1½ inches / 2–3 cm thick. Put aside.
- Wash the chanterelles to remove any soil, and chop them roughly.
- Heat some oil in a frying pan and sauté the chanterelles. Put aside.
- Meanwhile, heat a griddle over high heat and add the fillets. As the fillets are quite thick, you must decide how well done you want them. Two minutes of cooking on each side will give you rare meat. If you want it well done turn down the heat and cook it some more.
- Finally, transfer the meat to a plate, season with salt and pepper, and serve accompanied by the sautéed chanterelles.
- This dish serves 3.

PALEO-STYLE PREPARATION

- Thick fillets were cut from the hindquarters of a reindeer.
- Some chanterelles were picked and washed.
- A fire was prepared with wood from fir (*Abies alba*) and pine (*Pinus sylvestris* or *Pinus nigra*) trees. After being lit, it was left until the embers started to glow.
- The meat was placed straight on the embers and cooked for 30–45 minutes, depending on the intensity of the heat. The chanterelles were griddled at the same time.
- Once the meat was cooked, it would be removed along with the chanterelles from the fire and eaten straight away.

BONE MARROW OF AMERICAN BISON WITH RASPBERRIES

INGREDIENTS

- 1 American bison (*Bison bison*) or 1 femur of a calf (*Bos primogenius*)
- 12 wild raspberries (*Rubus idaeus*)

DID YOU KNOW THAT...?

Many long bones (femurs and tibias) have been found on archeological sites, deliberately broken so that their marrow could be removed and eaten. Bone marrow was probably widely used to feed young children whose mothers had stopped breastfeeding them though they could not yet eat much solid food. The widespread consumption of bone marrow 400,000 years ago is evident in Atapuerca, in Burgos, Spain. Wall paintings in the Cueva de Altamira, dating back 14,000 years, demonstrate the importance of the bison in the lives of the hunter-gatherers of the Magdalenean period.

Evidence of bison consumption has also been found on the German sites of Vogelherd and Bockstein-Törle.

MODERN PREPARATION

NB: *as the bones of an American bison are difficult to obtain, replace them with those of a calf.*

- Ask your butcher to split a calf's femur lengthwise. Leave it in water for 2 hours to prevent the marrow from turning black.
- Meanwhile, wash the raspberries and put aside in a bowl.
- After soaking the bone, remove the marrow and put aside in a bowl.
- You can wash the 2 pieces of bone again and use them as dishes to serve the raspberries and bone marrow in.

PALEO-STYLE PREPARATION

- If they had not hunted a bison, prehistoric people would have been able to obtain a dead one (or use any other type of bovine animal).
- Some wild raspberries would be gathered.
- The bison would be dismembered and the skin removed from a hind leg to separate the femur. The bones were broken with a sharp object and the marrow removed from them.
- The bone could be used as a plate, with the ingredients placed inside. The food would have been eaten with the hands.

REINDEER TONGUE WITH RASPBERRY SAUCE

INGREDIENTS

- 1 tongue of reindeer (*Rangifer tarandus*) or cow (*Bos primigenius taurus*)
- ½ cup / 40 g wild raspberries (*Rubus idaeus*)
- bay leaves (*Laurus nobilis*)
- thyme (*Thymus vulgaris*) (1 sprig)
- rosemary (*Rosmarinus officinalis*) (1 sprig)
- olive oil
- pepper
- salt

MODERN PREPARATION

NB: *a reindeer's tongue may be hard to find if this animal is not hunted in your area but you can use a calf's tongue instead.*

- Cook the tongue. Put it in a saucepan, covered with water. Season and add the bay leaves, thyme, and rosemary. Cover the saucepan and heat the water. Cook the tongue for 45 minutes after the water starts to boil.
- Meanwhile, make the raspberry sauce. Firstly, wash the raspberries and put aside for a while in a bowl to extract their juice. Then put them over low heat and stir gently but constantly for 25 minutes. After this time, transfer the sauce to a jar (you will have some left over, which can be kept for a few days in a refrigerator).
- Once the tongue is cooked, drain and peel it. Leave it to cool and then slice it to your preferred thickness. Season with a little salt and pepper.
- Put a little oil in a griddle or frying pan and sauté the tongue to taste.
- Transfer it to a serving plate and spread raspberry sauce on top of each slice.

PALEO-STYLE PREPARATION

- The tongue of a slaughtered reindeer would be sliced.
- Some raspberries would be picked and then beaten in water to obtain a runny paste.
- A piece of schist or another flat stone would be placed directly onto a fire and the tongue would be put on it. It would be cooked for 15–20 minutes (depending on the thickness of the tongue and individual choice). Raspberry paste could be added.
- The meat would be eaten as soon as it was ready.

DID YOU KNOW THAT...?

Domesticated reindeer were a good source of protein for the prehistoric inhabitants of the northern hemisphere.

Reindeer meat is succulent and tasty—as well as very nutritious, due to its high levels of minerals and low level of fat.

STONE-GRIDDLED GOAT'S LIVER WITH BAY LEAVES

INGREDIENTS

- ¼ liver of goat (*Capra aegagrus hircus*) or kid
- 4 bay leaves (*Laurus nobilis*)
- olive oil
- pepper
- salt

MODERN PREPARATION

- Slice the liver (or buy it ready sliced).
- Brush the liver slices with a little oil. Heat a griddle over high heat and cook the liver, along with the bay leaves, for 3–5 minutes, according to your taste.
- If the bay leaves start to burn, remove them from the griddle and add them again at the last minute.
- Once the liver is cooked, season it with salt and pepper. Serve it on a plate, inserting a bay leaf between each pair of liver slices.

PALEO-STYLE PREPARATION

- A wild goat would be hunted to obtain the liver.
- Some bay leaves would be picked.
- The liver would be sliced to the preferred thickness, using a flint knife or another suitable utensil.
- A sandwich would be made, using liver, bay leaf, liver in sequence.
- A fire (perhaps made with pine wood) would be built, and a piece of flat stone would be placed directly on it and heated. When hot, the liver sandwiches would be placed on the stone. They would take 5–10 minutes to cook.
- The food could be served on a cold piece of stone or on the stone it was cooked on.

DID YOU KNOW THAT...?

Liver was highly prized by prehistoric hunter-gatherers. Once they had hunted their prey, they used to eat the liver raw, while it was still warm. (The San people of Southern Africa continue this practice today.)

MOUSSE OF BONE MARROW WHISKED WITH STRAWBERRIES

INGREDIENTS

- 2 or 3 femur of a calf (*Bos primigenius taurus*)
- 12 wild strawberries (*Fragaria vesca*)
- 1 celery stalk (*Apium graveolens*)
- 1 bottle of mineral water

MODERN PREPARATION

- Ask your butcher to split a calf's femur lengthwise. Leave it in water for 2 hours to prevent the marrow from turning black.
- Meanwhile, wash the raspberries and put them aside in a strainer.
- Also wash the celery. Dry it and cut it into strips 2–2½ inches / 5–6 cm long.
- Once the bones have soaked, remove their marrow and put it into a blender.
- Add the strawberries and, little by little, the mineral water. Blend until you obtain the texture of a mousse.
- Serve the mousse in small wooden bowls as a dip, accompanied by the strips of celery.

PALEO-STYLE PREPARATION

- Our ancestors would easily be able to obtain some long bones with plenty of marrow inside.
- They would break the bones with a sharp instrument and remove the marrow.
- Wild strawberries would be picked and crushed, and they would also pick some celery stalks.
- The strawberries would be crushed with some water to obtain an even, runny mixture.
- The mixture would be placed in a receptacle and blended into the marrow. It would perhaps be drunk, using celery stalks as spoons.

DID YOU KNOW THAT...?

Bones found at the site of Cova de les Teixoneres Moià (Barcelona, Spain) help us to discover what cooking methods were used by the Neanderthals.

OX HEART WITH WILD MUSHROOMS

INGREDIENTS

- ½ ox heart (*Bos primigenius taurus*)
- 1¼ cups / 100 g sliced wild mushrooms (*Bolelus edulis*)
- rosemary, (*Rosmarinus officinalis*), ground + 1 sprig
- olive oil
- pepper
- salt

DID YOU KNOW THAT...?

Oxen were widely eaten on all the archeological sites from the Middle and Upper Pleistocene period. The last known oxen on the Iberian peninsula became extinct as a result of overhunting, probably around 7,000–8,000 years ago. As we have seen, Sota Palou (Girona, Spain) is one of the sites where wild boar were eaten—one of the last of its kind during the prehistory of the Pyrenees.

MODERN PREPARATION

- Slice the ox heart (or buy it ready sliced). Season with salt and pepper.
- Before slicing them, wash the mushrooms to remove any soil.
- Heat some oil in a frying pan, add the mushrooms, and sauté them.
- Meanwhile, brush the ox-heart slices with a little oil. Heat a griddle over high heat and cook them for 3–5 minutes (according to taste), along with the sprig of rosemary (to allow its flavor to impregnate the meat).
- Finally, serve the ox heart with the mushrooms and dust with a little ground rosemary to taste.

PALEO-STYLE PREPARATION

- An ox heart would be sliced with a flint knife or other appropriate utensil.
- The mushrooms would be picked, then washed and sliced.
- A fire would be made, if possible with oak and holm-oak wood. A piece of flat stone such as crystallized travertine would be placed on the fire.
- The ox-heart slices would be placed on this stone, along with the mushrooms, and cooked for 15 minutes.
- After this time, the stone would be removed from the fire. The ox heart was eaten, using a sharp stick in place of a fork.

GOAT KIDNEYS WITH FIGS

INGREDIENTS

- 1 kidney of a goat (*Capra aegagrus hircus*) or kid
- 6 figs (*Ficus carica*)
- olive oil
- salt
- vinegar

MODERN PREPARATION

- Firstly, wash the kidney and leave for 1 hour in water, vinegar, and a little salt, to eliminate the toxins. After this time, rinse the kidney under running water and dry it with kitchen paper.
- Slice the kidney very thinly and season with salt.
- Peel the figs and remove all their flesh. Put aside in a bowl.
- Heat a little oil in a griddle over high heat. Add the kidney slices. Avoid cooking them too much, to prevent them from drying out.
- Transfer the kidney slices to a serving plate and spread the figs on top.

PALEO-STYLE PREPARATION

- Our prehistoric ancestor would hunt a wild goat. Its kidney would be sliced very thinly.
- A handful of figs would be picked and peeled, and the flesh removed.
- To cook, a fire would be made and a stone put on top of it. When the stone was hot, the kidney slices would be placed on it and griddled.
- Once they were done, the figs would be spread on top and the meal would be eaten straight away.

DID YOU KNOW THAT...?

Figs have a high nutritional value as they contain many vitamins and minerals, as well as plenty of fiber. They also have laxative and anti-rheumatic properties.

CALF'S BRAIN
IN PARTRIDGE EGGS

INGREDIENTS

- 1 brain of a calf (*Bos primigenius taurus*)
- 6 red partridge (*Alectoris rufa*) eggs or quail (*Coturnix coturnix*) eggs
- green vegetables
- wild flowers
- olive oil
- salt

MODERN PREPARATION

NB: *partridge eggs are not available all the year around. They can be replaced by quail eggs.*

– Put the brain in a bowl, covered with cold water, for 2 hours, changing the water several times. The brain will turn white as it loses its blood. Then heat some salted water in a saucepan. When it starts to boil, add the brain and cook it for 5–7 minutes. After this time, transfer the brain to a bowl containing cold water. Remove it, and dry it on kitchen paper.

– Shell and whisk the eggs. If they prove difficult to shell, make a hole with a sharp knife—do not worry about breaking the yolk as in this recipe that does not matter.

– Dip the brain into the whisked eggs and fry it in hot oil. Then leave it on kitchen paper, to soak up the cooking oil.

– Wash the greens. Arrange them on a serving plate and place the brain on top. Garnish with wild flowers.

PALEO-STYLE PREPARATION

– A wild calf's brain and several partridge eggs would be obtained.

– The brain would be sliced, and the slices would be dipped in the whisked partridge eggs.

– A stone, preferably crystallized travertine, would be placed directly on top of a fire. When it was hot the brain slices would be griddled on it for about 15 minutes.

– Once they were cooked, they would be removed from the fire and eaten with some greens and wild flowers.

DID YOU KNOW THAT...?

We know if an animal has been eaten by humans by analyzing the cuts on its bones. This also tells us the type of tool used to prepare them for eating.

SPINACH AND FOREST FRUIT SALAD

INGREDIENTS

- 1 handful of spinach (*Spinacia oleracea*)
- 12 wild strawberries (*Fragaria vesca*)
- 12 blueberries (*Vaccinium myrtillus*)
- 24 sunflower seeds (*Helianthus annuus*)
- olive oil
- salt (optional)
- pepper (optional)
- vinegar (optional)

MODERN PREPARATION

- Wash the spinach and then dry it thoroughly to eliminate all the water. Transfer it to a bowl.
- Wash the strawberries and blueberries and add them to the spinach.
- Mix all the ingredients and then sprinkle the sunflower seeds on top.
- Finally, toss with oil and season to taste with salt and other condiments of your choice (pepper, vinegar, etc.).

PALEO-STYLE PREPARATION

- A handful of spinach, some wild strawberries and blueberries, and a dry sunflower head would be picked.
- The spinach, blueberries, and strawberries would be washed before being placed in a receptacle.
- The seeds were then removed from the sunflower. This could be done individually (a very slow process) or by gently pushing the back of the flower head upward with the fingers.
- A fire would be made and left until glowing embers could be seen. Then a stone was put on top. When it was very hot, the sunflower seeds were toasted on it until they became crunchy when opened. They were removed from the fire and peeled.
- Finally, the seeds would be sprinkled over the salad.

DID YOU KNOW THAT...?

We are omnivorous—in other words, our diet involves eating both meat and plants, including green leaves, forest fruits, and other edible plants.

Spinach has one of the highest protein levels of all plants and it abounds in fibers and vitamins. It also provides Omega-3 fatty acids.

LENTIL HUMMUS WITH CARROTS AND WILD MUSHROOMS

INGREDIENTS

- ½ cup / 100 g lentils (*Lens culinaris*)
- 4–5 small carrots (*Daucus carota*)
- 6 wild mushrooms
- 2 bay leaves (*Laurus nobilis*)
- 2 cloves of garlic (*Allium satvium*)
- cumin (*Cuminum cyninum*)
- sesame seeds (*Sesamum indicum*)
- olive oil
- pepper
- salt

MODERN PREPARATION

- Firstly, wash the lentils under running water and then drain them.
- Put the lentils in a saucepan with salted water and the bay leaves. Cook over medium heat for 30 minutes, or until the lentils are soft.
- Meanwhile, peel the carrots. Wash the wild mushrooms with just sufficient water to remove any soil, then chop them roughly.
- Cook the carrots in boiling water for 2–4 minutes, or until they are soft. Drain and put aside.
- Sauté the mushrooms in a frying pan with a few drops of oil. Season with salt when they are almost done. Put them aside and sprinkle with a little oil when you serve them.
- Once the lentils are cooked, drain them and transfer to a blender. Add a pinch each of salt, pepper, and cumin, as well as the chopped garlic, and blend them briefly. Add a generous squirt of oil and continue blending until smooth.
- Finally, transfer the lentil hummus to a small bowl and sprinkle with some sesame seeds and oil. Serve with the carrots and wild mushrooms.

PALEO-STYLE PREPARATION

- Paleolithic people would collect a good handful of lentils, a few bay leaves, some carrots, and some wild mushrooms. The soil would be washed from the carrots and mushrooms. They would be chopped roughly, leaving a few whole.
- A fire would be lit and a tripod set up over it.
- The lentils and bay leaves were put in a receptacle with water. This was hung from the tripod and the contents were boiled for 50–60 minutes.
- After this time, the receptacle was detached from the tripod and a piece of stone was heated on the fire. The wild mushrooms were cooked on the hot stone.
- Meanwhile the lentils were beaten into a purée.
- The whole carrots and whole wild mushrooms were used as eating utensils.

DID YOU KNOW THAT...?

Lentils have an abundance of B-group vitamins and are therefore useful for combatting anemia. They help prevent fatigue and are also good for the eyesight, memory, and bones, as well as boosting the immune system.

ROCKET SALAD WITH WILD STRAWBERRIES

INGREDIENTS

- 1 bunch of rocket (*Eruca vesicaria*)
- 12 wild strawberries (*Fragaria vesca*)
- 24 pine nuts (*Pinus pinea*)
- mint (*Mentha spp.*)
- wild flowers
- olive oil
- salt

MODERN PREPARATION

- Wash and drain the rocket and transfer it to a salad bowl.
- Wash the strawberries and add them to the bowl, along with the mint, chopped very finely.
- Brown the pine nuts in a frying pan. There is no need to add any oil as the nuts will release it themselves. Add them to the salad.
- Finally, season to taste with oil, salt, and any other desired condiments. Serve garnished with wild flowers.

PALEO-STYLE PREPARATION

- A bunch of rocket and some mint, pine cones, wild strawberries, and flowers were gathered on walks in the mountains.
- The rocket and the strawberries were washed and put into a receptacle.
- The mint was finely chopped and added to the other ingredients.
- Next the pine nuts were removed from the cones, peeled, and added to the salad.
- A garnish of a few wild flowers was added just before the food was eaten.

DID YOU KNOW THAT...?

Rocket is extremely healthy, as it is anti-carcinogenic and acts as a detoxicating agent. It also helps the body assimilate calcium and enhances digestion.

CARPACCIO OF SUMMER MUSHROOMS WITH FILBERTS

INGREDIENTS

- 4 large mushrooms (*Bolelus aestivalis*)
- 12 wild filberts (*Corylus avellana*)
- olive oil
- salt

MODERN PREPARATION

- Choose large mushrooms that are a good size for slicing.
- Slice them as thinly as possible and arrange them on the serving plate.
- Crush the filberts with a mortar and pestle until they are reduced to powder.
- Sprinkle the powdered nuts onto the mushroom slices.
- Before serving the salad, season with salt and drizzle on a little oil.

PALEO-STYLE PREPARATION

- Our ancestors would pick a small mushroom and a few wild filberts.
- They would slice the mushroom thinly with a flint knife.
- The filberts were crushed until they were reduced to powder.
- The powdered nuts were sprinkled onto the mushroom.
- Finally, the salad was eaten using the hands.

DID YOU KNOW THAT...?

In 2015 a study by the Max Planck Institute for Evolutionary Anthropology in Germany recorded the first evidence of the human consumption of wild mushrooms, dating back to the Upper Paleolithic Era. The evidence was derived from the examination of plant residues in teeth found in the Cueva del Mirón in Cantabria, Spain.

SCOTCH BONNET AND RASPBERRY SALAD

INGREDIENTS

- 50–60 Scotch bonnets (*Marasmius oreades*)
- 12 raspberries (*Rubus idaeus*)
- olive oil
- salt

MODERN PREPARATION

- Leave the Scotch bonnets to soak for 3–4 hours.
- Wash the raspberries and put them aside.
- Heat a little oil in a frying pan or griddle. Add the caps of the Scotch bonnets (discarding the stalks), season with salt, and sauté until they take on a darker color.
- Transfer them to a serving plate and add the raspberries.

PALEO-STYLE PREPARATION

- Spring is the time to pick Scotch bonnets. They grow in clusters in fields and the open countryside.
- Prehistoric people would pick perhaps 50–60 Scotch bonnets, as well as a handful of raspberries.
- They would remove the stalks of the mushrooms, and mix the caps with the raspberries. The salad would be eaten using the hands.

DID YOU KNOW THAT...?

Scotch bonnets are ideally suited to a low-sodium diet. They contain high levels of minerals such as potassium, iron, and phosphorus.

PURSLANE SALAD WITH WALNUTS, FIGS, AND WILD STRAWBERRY SAUCE

INGREDIENTS

- 1 cup / 100 g purslane (*Portulaca oleracea*)
- 4 walnuts (*Juglans regia*) chopped into pieces
- 2 figs (*Ficus carica*)

FOR THE STRAWBERRY SAUCE
- 1 cup / 200 g strawberries (*Fragaria vesca*)
- 2½ tbsp / 40 ml water

MODERN PREPARATION

- *To make the strawberry sauce:* heat some water, and when it starts to boil add the strawberries. Cook them until they are soft. Put them in a blender to obtain a thin sauce. Put aside.
- Remove the roots of the purslane (this can be done easily with your hands), carefully wash the leaves to remove any traces of soil, and then leave them to dry.
- Once they are dry, put them in a salad bowl, and add the walnut pieces and figs (split into 2).
- Add the strawberry sauce as a dressing.

PALEO-STYLE PREPARATION

- Purslane would be gathered beside tracks, along with some walnuts, figs, and wild strawberries.
- The stalks would be removed from the strawberries and the roots from the purslane. The walnuts would be shelled and chopped using a heavy object.
- The purslane would be soaked in water for 20 minutes. Then it was removed from the water and left to dry.
- Meanwhile, the strawberries were beaten into a purée with a little water.
- Finally, the purslane was put on a fig or banana leaf, the walnut pieces and figs (split into 2) were added, and the strawberry purée was poured on top.

DID YOU KNOW THAT...?

Purslane is rich in Omega-3 fatty acids and is an excellent source of vitamins. It also has various medicinal properties, as it is analgesic and anti-inflammatory. It is a blood tonic and is effective against arthritis and headaches.

WARM CHANTERELLE, PEAR, AND POMEGRANATE SALAD

INGREDIENTS

- 12 chanterelles (*Cantharellus cibarius*)
- 1 pear (*Pyrus communis*)
- 1 pomegranate (*Punica granatum*)
- olive oil
- salt

MODERN PREPARATION

- Firstly, wash, dry, and chop the chanterelles. Also wash the pear.
- Remove the pomegranate seeds. There is a very simple way to do this. Cut the pomegranate in half and beat the skin with the convex side of a spoon to detach the seeds from the shell, allowing them to fall into a bowl or plate. Put aside.
- Sauté the chanterelles in a frying pan with a little oil, and then season with salt. Remove the frying pan from the heat, but leave the chanterelles inside so that they stay warm.
- Cut the unpeeled pear into 4, remove the core, and slice.
- Transfer the chanterelles to a serving plate, sprinkle with the pomegranate seeds, and decorate with the pear slices.

PALEO-STYLE PREPARATION

- Our ancestors would gather a handful of chanterelles, a pear, and a pomegranate.
- They would chop the mushrooms and wash the pieces, then remove the seeds of the pomegranate. Finally, they would wash and slice the pear.
- They would make a fire and, when the embers started to glow, heat a piece of stone on it. The chanterelles were placed on the stone and cooked.
- The stone was removed from the fire and the pomegranate seeds and the pear slices were added to it.
- This could be eaten straight away as a warm salad.

DID YOU KNOW THAT…?

Chanterelles, like other wild mushrooms, constitute a light food rich in group-B vitamins and minerals (particularly potassium and phosphorus).

MUSHROOMS WITH MADRONE BERRIES

INGREDIENTS

- 1–2 mushrooms (*Macro-lepiota procera*)
- 12 madrone (*Arbutus unedo*) berries
- olive oil
- salt

MODERN PREPARATION

- Remove the mushroom stalks and wash the caps.
- Wash the madrone berries and put aside.
- Heat a little oil in a frying pan or griddle. Add the mushrooms and sauté them until they take on a darker color. Season with salt at the last minute.
- Transfer them to a serving plate and add the madrone berries, which can be served whole or in pieces.

PALEO-STYLE PREPARATION

- Our prehistoric ancestors would pick some mushrooms and madrone berries. Then they were washed, along with the madrone berries.
- A piece of flat stone, such as schist, was placed on a fire. Once it was hot, the mushrooms were added and cooked.
- The mushrooms were mixed with the madrone berries and the food was eaten with the hands.

DID YOU KNOW THAT...?

Madrone berries help prevent cardiovascular and degenerative diseases, as well as being good for the circulation.

GRAPE AND BLACKBERRY SALAD

INGREDIENTS

- small bunch of grapes (*Vitis vinifera*)
- 24 blackberries (*Morus nigra*)

MODERN PREPARATION

- – Wash the grapes and blackberries.
- – Drain and dry them thoroughly.
- – If you prefer, you can peel the grapes and remove their seeds.
- – Mix the grapes and blackberries in a bowl to create a variant of the classic fruit salad.

PALEO-STYLE PREPARATION

- – Ancient people would pick a small bunch of wild or domesticated grapes.
- – They would also gather 2 dozen or so ripe blackberries (ideally at the beginning of September).
- – The grapes and blackberries would be washed.
- – The fruits would be mixed and eaten together.

DID YOU KNOW THAT...?

The excavations in the Wonderwerk Cave in South Africa have revealed evidence of grape eating in prehistoric times.

CARROT, PINE NUT, AND RASPBERRY SALAD

INGREDIENTS

- 2 carrots (*Daucus carota*) (1 of them black or purple)
- 12 raspberries (*Rubus idaeus*)
- 6 tbsp / 50 g pine nuts (*Pinus pinea*)
- olive oil
- salt

MODERN PREPARATION

– Wash and peel the carrots, and then cut them into thin slices. Drizzle them with oil and season with salt. Put aside.

– Wash and dry the raspberries. Put aside.

– Toast the pine nuts in a frying pan until they turn golden. You will not need any oil for this as the pine nuts will release their own. Put aside.

– Finally, put the carrot, raspberries, and pine nuts on a serving plate. The different colors of the carrots make this dish visually striking and highly appetizing.

PALEO-STYLE PREPARATION

– Some carrots would be gathered, washed, peeled, and chopped.

– Then a pine cone would be foraged for. The pine nuts would be removed from it and peeled.

– Some bark would be found to use as a plate for the carrots, pine nuts, and raspberries.

DID YOU KNOW THAT...?

The archeological site of La Draga in Banyoles, Girona (Spain), has shown that fruits and berries were picked from the nearby woods 7,000 years ago. These include walnuts, pine nuts, blackberries, sloes, and wild apples and pears.

SLOE AND APPLE SALAD WITH MADRONE SAUCE

INGREDIENTS

- 12 sloes (*Prunus spinosa*)
- 1 apple (*Malus domestica*)
- 12 madrone (*Arbustus unedo*) berries
- 12 filberts (*Corylus avellana*)

FOR THE MADRONE SAUCE
- 1 cup / 250 g of madrone berries
- 3½ tbsp / 50 ml of water

MODERN PREPARATION

- *To make the madrone sauce:* wash the madrone berries and remove their stalks. Heat some water. When it starts to boil, add the madrone berries (putting aside a few whole berries). Stir continuously with a wooden spoon until the berries are soft. Transfer them to a blender and then strain them to remove the seeds. Put aside.
- Wash the apple (unpeeled), cut it into 4, and then slice it. Also wash the sloes.
- Crush the filberts in a mortar.
- Brown the apple slices slightly in a griddle with a few drops of oil. Transfer them to a serving plate.
- Serve accompanied by the sloes and whole berries. Drizzle on the madrone sauce.

PALEO-STYLE PREPARATION

- A wild apple would be picked by prehistoric people along with some sloes, madrone berries, and filberts.
- The filberts were crushed.
- A few madrone berries were left whole. The remainder were beaten in a little water until a thin purée was obtained.
- The apple would then be sliced with a flint knife.
- The apple would be eaten with the whole berries, sloes, filbert pieces, and madrone sauce.

INDEX

CHESTNUTS
antelope cooked on embers with chestnuts **94**
wild boar stew with bay leaves and chestnuts **82**
pheasant with chestnuts **60**

CHICKEN
eggs cooked on embers **22**

CHIVES
stone-fried ostrich egg with chives **20**

CLAMS
steamed with celery **34**
stone-griddled with partridge **32**

COW BONES
bone marrow of American bison with
raspberries **100**
mousse of bone marrow whisked with
strawberries **106**

CRAB
freshwater crabs cooked on embers with thyme **40**
scrambled partridge eggs with crabs and
asparagus **42**
stone-griddled crabs with garlic and bay leaves **44**

CUMIN
lentil hummus with carrots and wild
mushrooms **116**

D
DEER
antelope cooked on embers with chestnuts **94**
venison steak with green beans and carrots **84**

DILL
smoked salmon **48**

E
EGGS
calf's brain in partridge eggs **112**
chicken eggs **22**
cooked on embers **22**
goose eggs **22**
hamburger with false ketchup, mustard,
and onion **86**
partridge eggs with sloes **18**

quail eggs **22**
scrambled partridge eggs with crabs and
asparagus **42**
stone-fried ostrich egg with chives **20**

F
FENNEL
skewered salmon with fennel **46**

FIGS
baked trout stuffed with strawberries and
accompanied by red fruits **52**
goat kidneys with figs **110**
purslane salad with walnuts, figs, and wild
strawberry sauce **124**

FILBERTS
carpaccio of summer mushrooms with filberts **120**
sloe and apple salad with madrone sauce **134**
trout with rosemary and nuts **50**

G
GARLIC
guinea-fowl with garlic **64**
lentil hummus with carrots and wild
mushrooms **116**
roast reindeer with garlic and thyme **96**
roast wild boar with red fruit sauce **80**
stone-griddled crabs with garlic and bay leaves **44**

GOAT
grilled rack of goat **72**
skewered goat **70**
stone-griddled goat's liver with bay leaves **104**

GOOSE
eggs cooked on embers **22**
with olives **66**

GRAPES
grape and blackberry salad **130**
mussels with grapes **36**

GREEN BEANS
venison steak with green beans and carrots **84**

GREEN-NECKED DUCK
goose with olives **66**

GUINEA-FOWL
with garlic **64**

H
HEART
ox heart with wild mushrooms **108**

HUMMUS
lentil hummus with carrots and wild
mushrooms **116**

J
JUNIPER
stone-griddled tuna fish with juniper and rocket **58**

K
KETCHUP (FALSE)
hamburger with false ketchup, mustard,
and onion **86**

KID
goat kidneys with figs **110**
grilled rack of goat **72**
reindeer cooked on embers with chanterelles **98**
roast reindeer with garlic and thyme **96**
skewered goat **70**
stone-griddled goat's liver with bay leaves **104**

KIDNEYS
goat kidneys with figs **110**

L
LARD
beef stew with walnut and apple **88**
goose with olives **66**
guinea-fowl with garlic **64**
pheasant with chestnuts **60**
pigeon stuffed with red fruits **62**
roast wild boar with forest fruit sauce **80**
wild boar stew with bay leaves and chestnuts **82**

LAVENDER
frogs with lavender **136**

LEMON
mussels with grapes **36**

LENTILS
lentil hummus with carrots and wild
mushrooms **116**

LIVER
stone-griddled goat's liver with bay leaves **104**

M
MADRONE BERRIES
baked trout stuffed with strawberries and
accompanied by red fruits **52**
mushrooms with madrone berries **128**
pigeon stuffed with red fruits **62**

MINT
razor clams boiled with mint **30**
rocket salad with wild strawberries **118**
smoked salmon **48**
snails cooked on embers with mint **24**

MUSSELS
smoked **38**
with grapes **36**

MUSTARD
hamburger with false ketchup, mustard,
and onion **86**
trout with mustard **54**

N
NEPTUNE GRASS
smoked mussels **38**

O
OLIVES
goose with olives **66**

OX
ox heart with wild mushrooms **108**

P

PARTRIDGE
calf's brain in partridge eggs **112**
eggs with sloes **18**
pigeon stuffed with red fruits **62**
scrambled partridge eggs with crabs and
asparagus **42**

PEAR
hamburger with false ketchup, mustard,
and onion **86**
warm chanterelle, pear, and pomegranate
salad **126**

PHEASANT
with chestnuts **60**

PIGEON
stuffed with red fruits **62**

PINE NUTS
carrot, pine nut, and raspberry salad **132**
rocket salad with wild strawberries **118**
trout with rosemary and nuts **50**
tuna fish cooked on embers with pine nuts **56**

POMEGRANATE
antelope cooked on embers with chestnuts **94**
warm chanterelle, pear, and pomegranate
salad **126**

PORK
venison steak with green beans and carrots **84**

PURSLANE
baked trout stuffed with strawberries and
accompanied by red fruits **52**
purslane salad with walnuts, figs, and wild
strawberry sauce **124**

Q

QUAIL
calf's brain in partridge eggs **112**
eggs **18, 22**
stone-griddled clams with quail **32**

R

RABBIT
stone-griddled snails with rabbit **26**
with herbs **68**

RASPBERRIES
baked trout stuffed with strawberries and
accompanied by red fruits **52**
bone marrow of American bison with
raspberries **100**
carrot, pine nut, and raspberry salad **132**
pigeon stuffed with red fruits **62**
reindeer tongue with raspberry sauce **102**
Scotch bonnet and raspberry salad **122**

RAZOR CLAMS
boiled with mint **30**
with rosemary **28**

RED FRUITS
baked trout stuffed with strawberries and
accompanied by red fruits **52**
hamburger with false ketchup, mustard,
and onion **86**
pigeon stuffed with red fruits **62**
roast wild boar with red fruit sauce **80**

REINDEER
cooked on embers with chanterelles **98**
reindeer tongue with raspberry sauce **102**
roasted with garlic and thyme **96**

ROCKET
grilled rack of goat **72**
hamburger with false ketchup, mustard,
and onion **86**
rocket salad with wild strawberries **118**
stone-griddled tuna fish with juniper berries and
rocket **58**

ROSEMARY
ox heart with wild mushrooms **108**
rabbit with herbs **68**
razor clams with rosemary **28**
reindeer tongue with raspberry sauce **102**
roast wild boar with red fruit sauce **80**
skewered goat **70**
stone-grilled snails with rabbit **26**
trout with rosemary and nuts **50**

S

SALAD
carrot, pine nut, and raspberry salad **132**
grape and blackberry salad **130**
purslane salad with walnuts, figs, and wild
strawberry sauce **124**
rocket with wild strawberries **118**
Scotch bonnet and raspberry salad **122**
sloe and apple salad with madrone sauce **134**
spinach and forest fruit salad **114**
warm chanterelle, pear, and pomegranate
salad **126**

SALMON
skewered salmon with fennel **46**
smoked salmon **48**

SCOTCH BONNET
Scotch bonnet and raspberry salad **122**

SESAME
lentil hummus with carrots and wild
mushrooms **116**

SLOES
baked trout stuffed with strawberries and
accompanied by red fruits **52**
eggs with sloes **18**
pigeon stuffed with red fruits **62**
sloe and apple salad with madrone sauce **134**

SMOKED SALT
smoked salmon **48**

SNAILS
cooked on embers with mint **24**
stone-griddled with rabbit **26**

SNAP PEAS
smoked strips of wild boar with snap peas **76**

SPINACH
spinach and forest fruit salad **114**

SPROUTS
calf's brain in partridge eggs **112**

SUMMER MUSHROOMS
carpaccio of summer mushrooms with filberts **120**

SUNFLOWER SEEDS
spinach and forest fruit salad **114**

T

THYME
freshwater crabs cooked on embers **40**
goose with olives **66**
roast reindeer with garlic and thyme **96**

TONGUE
reindeer tongue with raspberry sauce **102**

TROUT
baked trout stuffed with strawberries and
accompanied by red fruits **52**
with mustard **54**
with rosemary and nuts **50**

TUNA FISH
cooked on embers with pine nuts **56**
stone-griddled tuna fish with juniper berries and
rocket **58**

W

WAKAME
smoked mussels **38**

WALNUTS
beef stew with walnuts and apple **88**
purslane salad with walnuts, figs, and wild
strawberry sauce **124**

WILD BOAR
griddled with apple compote **78**
roast with red fruit sauce **80**
smoked strips of wild boar with snap peas **76**
stew with bay leaves and chestnuts **82**

WILD FLOWERS
calf's brain in partridge eggs **112**
rocket salad with wild strawberries **118**

WILD MUSHROOMS
carpaccio of summer mushrooms with filberts **120**
lentil hummus with carrots and wild
mushrooms **116**

mushrooms with madrone berries **128**
ox heart with wild mushrooms **108**
reindeer cooked on embers with chanterelles **98**
Scotch bonnet and raspberry salad **122**
warm chanterelle, pear, and pomegranate
salad **126**

WILD STRAWBERRIES
beef steak with wild strawberries **90**
grilled rack of goat **72**
mousse of bone marrow whisked with
strawberries **106**

BIBLIOGRAPHY

AIELLO, L.; WHEELER, P. «The Expensive-Tissue Hypothesis: The Brain and the Digestive System in Human and Primate Evolution». *Current Anthropology*, 36 (1995), pp. 199–221.

ARSUAGA, J. L.; MARTÍNEZ, I. La especie elegida. *La larga marcha de la evolución humana*. Madrid: Temas de Hoy, 1998.

BARTON, R. N. E.; CURRANT, A. P.; FERNÁNDEZ-JALVO, Y.; FINLAYSON, J. C.; GOLDBERG, P.; MACPHAIL, R.; PETTIT, P. B.; STRINGER, C. B. «Gibraltar Neanderthals and results of recent excavations in Gorham's, Vanguard and Ibex Caves». *Antiquity*, 73 (1999), pp. 13–23.

BERMÚDEZ DE CASTRO, J. M. *El Chico de la Gran Dolina. En los orígenes de lo humano*. Barcelona: Crítica, 2002.

BUXÓ, R. *Arqueología de las plantas. La explotación económica de las semillas y los frutos en el marco mediterráneo de la península Ibérica*. Barcelona: Crítica, 1997.

BUXÓ, R. «La reconstrucció de la vegetació prehistòrica. El cas de llavors i fruits a Catalunya». *Cota Zero*, 4 (1988), pp. 39–45.

BUXÓ, R. «Recherches sur les données carpologiques du site de Lattes (Hérault)», D.E.A. en *Histoire et Civilizations* Académie de Montpellier, 1988.

CARBONELL, E.; BERMÚDEZ DE CASTRO, J. M.; ARSUAGA, J. L.; DÍEZ, J. C.; ROSAS, A.; CUENCA-BESCOS, G.; SALA, R.; MOSQUERA, M.; RODRÍGUEz, X. P. «Lower Pleistocene Hominids and Artifacts from Atapuerca-TD6 (Spain)». *Science*, 269 (1995), pp. 826–832.

FLOUEST, A.; ROMAC, J-P. (2011). *La cocina neolítica y la cueva de La Molle-Pierra*. Gijón: Ed. Trea, 2011.

GOREN INBAR, N.; ALPERSON, N.; KISLEY, M. E.; SIMCHONI, O.; MELAMED, Y.; BEN-NUN, A.; WERKER, E. «Evidence of Hominin Control of Fire at Gesher Benot Ya'aqov». *Science*, 304 (2002), pp. 725–727.

GRINE, F. «Dental evidence for dietary differences in Australopithecus and Paranthropus: a quantitative analysis of permanent molar microwear». *Journal of Human Evolution*, 15 (1986), pp. 783–822.

GRINE F.; KAY, R. «Early hominid diets from quantitative image analysis of dental microwear». *Nature*, 333 (1988), pp. 765–768.

HANSEN, J. M. *The Paleoethnobotany of Franchthi Cave*, Greece. Ph. D. Thesis. University of Minnesota. University Microfilms International: Ann Arbor, 1988.

HEINZELIN DE J. CLARK, J. D.; WHITE, T.; HART, W.; RENNE, P.; WOLDEGABRIEL, G.; BEYENE, Y.; VRBA, E. «Environment and Behavior of 2.5-Million-Year-Old Bouri Hominids». *Science*, 284 (1999), pp. 625–629.

HILLMAN, G. C. COLLEDGE, S. M.; HARRIS, D. R. 1989. «Plant-food economy during the Epipalaeolithic period at Tell Abu Hureyra, Syria: dietary diversity, seasonality, and modes of exploitation». En: HILLMAN, G. C. [ed.]. *Foraging and Farming:*

The Evolution of Plant Exploitation. Londres: Unwin Hyman, 1989, pp. 241–268.

JÄGER, K. D.; SCHÄFER. D. K. «Gathering Fruits as a Way of Food Supply During the Palaeolithic Period». En: EBH ULLRICH [ed.]. *Hominid Evolution. Lifestyles and Survival Strategies*. Gelsenkirchen / Schwelm: Archaea, 1999, pp. 429–434.

KAPLAN, H.; HILL, K.; LANCASTER, J.; HURTADO, A. M. «A Theory of Human Life History Evolution: Diet, Intelligence, and Longevity». *Evolutionary Anthropology*, 9 (2000), pp. 156–84.

MARINVAL, P. «Cueillette, agriculture et alimentation végétale de l'Épipaleolithique jusqu'au 2°. Age du Fer en France méridionale». París: Thèse pour le Doctorat, École des Hautes Études en Sciences Sociales, 1988.

MARINVAL, P. «La Balma Margineda. Cueillete et agriculture». *Les Dossiers, Histoire et Archéologie*, 96 (1985), pp. 147–150.

MERCADER, J.; PANGER, M.; BOESCH, C. «Excavation of a Chimpanzee Stone Tool Site in the African Rainforest». *Science*, 296 (2002), pp. 1452–1455.

PUECH, P-F.; ALBERTINI, H. «Dental Microwear and Mechanisms in Early Hominids From Laetoli and Hadar». *American Journal of Physical Anthropology*, 65 (1984), pp. 87–91.

PUECH, P-F.; CIANFARANI, F.; RIBOT ,F. «Maxillary Canine Microwear in Dryopithecus from Spain». *American Journal of Physical Anthropology*, 80 (1989), pp. 305–312.

RAGIR, S. «Diet and Food Preparation: Rethinking Early Hominid Behavior». *Evolutionary Anthropology*, 9 (2000), pp. 153–155.

SALAS-SALVADÓ, J.; ROS, E.; SABATÉ, J. [ed.]. *Frutos secos, salud y culturas mediterráneas*. Barcelona: Glosa, S.L., 2005.

SKOFLEK, I. «Plant Remains from the Vértessszöllös Travertine». En: KRETZOI, M.; DOBOSI, V. T. *Vértesszöllös: Man, Site and Culture*. Budapest: Akadémai Kiadó [ed.], 1990, pp. 77–123.

SPONHEIMER, M.; LEE-THORP J. A. «Isotopic Evidence for the Diet of an Early Hominid, *Australopithecus africanus*». *Science*, 238 (1999), pp. 368–370.

VAQUER, J.; GEDDES, D.; BARBAZA, M.; ERROUX, J. «Mesolithic plant exploitation at de Balma Abeurador (France)». *Oxford Journal of Archaeology*, 5 (1986), pp. 1–18.

WRANGHAM, R. W.; HOLLAND JONES, J.; LADEN, G.; PILBEAM, D.; CONKLIN-BRITTAIN, N. «The Raw and the Stolen. Cooking and the Ecology of Human Origins». *Current Anthropology*, 40 (1999), pp. 567–594.

ACKNOWLEDGEMENTS

To Francesc Burjachs, for his suggestions and advice about edible plants from the Paleolithic Era, and for his book list. Without his help it would have been very difficult to have had solid information about the chronology revealed by the study of pollens.

To Ethel Allué, for her expertise in carpology (the study of carbon fossils) and for the books she lent us.

To Xosé-Pedro Rodríguez, for clarifying our doubts about Australasia.

To Javier Fernández for supplying us with the names of archeological sites associated with malacofauna.

To Ignasi Pastó, for recommending articles and books on prehistoric eating habits.

To Hugues-Alexandre Blain, for the microfauna.

To Edgar Camarós, for information about German archeological sites.

To Manuel Vaquero, for clarifying the anthropization of some animal remains on archeological sites.